PASSPORT TO PARIS

À Kathy qui est charmante,

Glynne

PASSPORT TO PARIS

a memoir

GLYNNE HILLER

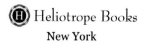 Heliotrope Books
New York

Parts of this memoir were published in slightly different form in *The Easthampton Star* and *The Nonbinary Review*.

Cover Design by Naomi Rosenblatt
Typeset by Naomi Rosenblatt with AJ&J Design

To Cathy

Chapter One

Sally's phone in Greenwich, Connecticut, rang five times before I heard her breathless voice. "Glynne?" she said. "I know it's you. Who else would call after eleven at night?"

"Only me," I agreed. I always turned to my sister Sally in times of travail. She was three years older than I and much more practical.

"Irving is asleep," she said, "and I had to scramble from my cozy warm bed and run downstairs to stop the blasted thing from waking him. So, are you all right, darling?"

"So-so. No, I'm okay. Sal, I can't talk for long. Joe will be home at any moment. I wasn't going to let you in on this because I know you'll groan, and I can just see the expression on your face. But you know I can't keep secrets from you, and anyway, you might not react the way I think you will."

"Oh, Glynne. What mad thing have you done now?"

"Nothing yet . . . possibly tonight."

"Tonight what?"

"Sal! We've had so many heart-to-heart talks about our husbands, and you've heard me blow hot and cold about Joe. Well, I'm on the cusp of a decision. I'm going to suggest a temporary separation, to see—"

"No, no! I don't want to hear."

"Oh, Sal. Don't just dismiss something because you don't like hearing about it. Living without Joe may sound drastic, but I want to try it, perhaps just for a couple of months, to help me learn what my true feelings are. Cathy, of course, will come with me."

"Oh God, Glynne. Do you imagine that inhabiting a different apartment will solve anything? Utter rubbish! If it turns out you're lonely in your new place, you'll suddenly realize how much you love Joe. But should a bevy of fascinating men be ready to squire you around . . . I don't want you to lose Joe. He's one in a million. The problem is you take him for granted. If he were single, there'd be a line of women panting after him."

"Possibly."

"I'm skeptical about hurtful confrontations. That one you indulged in last year wasn't a merry show. Anyhow, one thing is sure. It's simply not cricket to bash him over the head when he gets home late from work with stuff about a separation."

"Yet I need to have a straight talk with him."

"But you're not being fair. *You* may feel better after regurgitating, but darling, all your uncertainty threatens his manhood. You could wreck your life with one wrong turn. He adores you and Cathy. So don't be an impetuous chump!"

"Impetuous? Hardly. It's been on my mind for ages, and—"

"Really, Glynne! Only three weeks ago, when you called after that big soirée, you were ecstatic, telling me how Joe had been the life of the party, how you couldn't stop laughing, even though you'd heard most of his stories before. And then you went on and on about what fun it was dancing with him, dipping and gliding. You told me your two bodies felt like one."

"Well, I had fun, an evening out. But most of the time he's either at work or at Party meetings or teaching his adult education classes. Of course I'm really fond of him, but maybe I'm not in love with the guy."

"Oh, please." Sally's arm would now be shooting upward. "You, with a peach of a guy who's crazy about you and your lovely child. Unlike most husbands—Irving included—who resent their wives studying, Joe actually helps you choose which courses to take. And, okay, like most of us you're on a budget, but you're definitely not poor. In fact, you're the luckiest of ducks. Your trouble is that you expect full-time ecstasy."

"Well, I can't explain everything right now on the phone."

"Does that chap you met in Prague last year—what's his name?— have anything to do with it? I hope that little infatuation is over. When you're writing a newspaper piece in a city like Prague, everything is bound to seem dripping with violins and romance."

"His name is Schuyler, and I was doing two newspaper pieces, one in Prague and one in London."

"Yes, and who provided the contacts for both of your articles? And who insisted you go abroad, even if he had to take care of Cathy, alone? Your Joe."

"But Sally, my wanting to live apart from Joe for a while has nothing to do with Schuyler. He was being trained for leadership in the Communist Party and couldn't be seen publicly with me, an English woman, anyway. We didn't even have a common language. The only word of Czech I learned was *na shledanou*, which means good-bye. This hardly moved the relationship forward."

Sally giggled.

"I was aware from the start," I said, "that I could never be with Schuyler."

"And you were absolutely right."

A silence followed

"Sally, are you suggesting I spend the rest of my life with a wonderful guy who I'm not in love with? Is that your good advice?"

"I won't stoop to answer." Her voice was cool.

"Oh well. Call it *pax*."

When we were growing up in England, this monosyllable had invariably restored law and order to the most furious battles between my sisters and brothers. In 1939, when the War started, our father moved our family from Manchester, England, to Brooklyn, New York.

Now Sally said, "Okay, *pax* it is, darling. But you do go overboard easily. It's part of your charm. And getting back to you and Joe, your so-called straight talk could be catastrophic. Once voiced, those words and their reverberations are forever in the air.

"Remember those dances you went to when you were sixteen, how you'd come home in raptures. 'At last,' you'd caw, 'I've met a man who really understands me.' You remained delirious for a couple of weeks. Then your eyes would start to roll upward at the sound of his name and you'd say, 'What did I ever see in that dull clod?'"

It was true, and a bit funny. But I didn't want to laugh away what was haunting me now. "Well, I'm twenty-five now, and—"

I heard the key in the lock.

"Sally, I've got to go. Joe's here."

"Promise me one thing, Glynne. Soft-pedal whatever you were going to say. Be fair. Joe's tired and glad to be home. Cut out the temporary-separation bit. Please."

"Well, I'll try. Anyway, cheerio for now."

Although Sally and I had lived in the States since I was sixteen, we still sounded English and probably always would.

Joe walked in.

Chapter Two

Joe dropped his briefcase and kissed me briefly while kicking the door shut with his foot. "Hello, sweetheart. What are you doing up so late? You've got to be up early with Cathy, remember? I've got a meeting."

"I know."

His eyes behind his glasses were tired. It would be cruel to bring up the "us" conversation now.

"And how's Cath? What did our wonderful girl do today?" He hung his jacket in the closet.

"What did she do? She did the things all happy three-year-olds do. She sang 'The Old Gray Goose Is Dead' and all the Burl Ives songs, belting them out with all her might along with him on the record while crayoning all the time. And I taught her something new: how to walk on the top of the sofa, then jump down and bounce onto the cushions. It made her hysterical. She was laughing and shrieking 'More! More!'"

"Who wouldn't want to jump down on the sofa? I'm jealous!" He walked toward Cathy's room. "Gotta see that sweet bundle. Be back in a minute."

I was glad to have confided in Sally.

Joe returned. "She's got a new way of sleeping," he said. "Presses her nose deep in the pillow." With fake solemnity he added, "Mrs. Nahem, might this sleep posture indicate latent insecurity?" He knit his brows. "Ah! But what an adorable peach." He sat beside me.

"Much smarter than a peach. Joe, what made you so late tonight?"

"It was a madhouse at the office." He slid his eyes from side to side, a trick he'd mastered from Groucho Marx, his movie idol. "Fink, that fathead, kept me late at the office, and the class I teach at the Jefferson School is at eight, remember?"

The Jefferson School of Social Science was an adult education arm of the Communist Party U.S.A.

"So I didn't even have time to buy a Mars bar before my class. Gee! What a horse's ass that Fink is!"

He was referring to his boss, Charles Finkelston, a renowned lawyer.

"Oh, Joe, I'm sorry."

He bent over to kiss my cheek. "His stinginess—what you call 'mingyness'. . . " He shook his head. "Can you conceive of a fat man of seventy scrabbling on all fours after a thumbtack he'd dropped?"

"What actually made me late, though, happened after my class was over. I'd grabbed my briefcase and was dashing out when a student, a guy about sixty, tapped my shoulder. 'Teacher! I know it's late, sir, but when you said that capitalism is worse in some ways than feudalism, can you explain that?' So . . . " Joe sighed and raised his palms.

I understood. His explanation would not have been quick. It never was. I could see him droning on about the oppression of the worker, tying it into Karl Marx's theory of surplus value. I couldn't help smiling.

"Gotta eat," he said. Soon he was propelling me down the hall toward the kitchen, where he sliced himself a piece of coconut cake. We sat on high stools facing each other. "I even compared the changes from animal farming to animal factories, how the—" Catching the look in my eyes, he stopped. "Hey, *I'm* supposed to be the tired one, but I'm putting you to sleep."

Standing to pull out glasses from the cupboard, he recited, "A jug of milk, a piece of cake, and thou beside me. After which, we'll hoof it to bed." Chewing, he closed his eyes. "Mmm! Good cake."

I didn't mean to, but I blurted, "Listen, Joe. You're really such a dear; a good man, too, but with it all, the thing is . . . I'm not a hundred per cent sure I'm in love with you."

He was silent at first. Then he said confidently, "Well, you are. So don't be ridiculous."

"Remember our sessions with Dr. Kandler last year?" I asked. There had been six of them.

"They were effective," he said. "And we've had a pretty good marriage since then."

"We have, mainly. Do you remember how strongly he felt against our separating?"

"You're darn tootin'! Glynne, Kandler was on the ball."

I plunged on. "So we never tried one. Joe, for me it would have been a chance to stand on my own feet for the first time in my life. First I lived with my parents, and then we got married and I lived with you." I took a breath. "It's very tempting to go on being taken care of, to have things arranged for me, to live with a wonderful man. And you *are* wonderful. Yet there are times when I question everything."

"Everything?" His tone was sarcastic. "For example?"

"Well, okay. Politically, I'm left. But I'm not a Communist. I can't forgive the Soviet Union's nonaggression pact with Nazi Germany. But you justify it."

He reached for my hand. "We don't have to see eye-to-eye on everything. And you know, you tend to exaggerate, saying things about us you don't actually mean. Then something happens, and it's like turning a page, and you're my own Glynne again."

He pulled out his pipe, tamped a clump of tobacco in the bowl, and struck a match. After throwing his head back and exhaling, he said, "We're better off talking things out tomorrow, when we're fresh."

He paused. A pulse began twitching near his cheekbone. Abruptly, my eyes started to prickle. He said, "There's just one question. Give me a yes -or-no answer. Is there another man?"

"No. Nobody else."

"Then no sudden urgency?"

"No." But I couldn't stop myself. "I was seventeen when we got married—too young, I think. And then we were apart during the War. I'm twenty-five now. I've changed."

"You think you've changed and I haven't? Nonsense. The seeds of who we are stay with us." He paused. "Wisdom from a philosophy major." He winked, then started chewing his bottom lip.

Did this gesture mean he was deliberating, or was he concealing anger?

Slowly I said, "Joe, I'm wondering if a short separation—"

"Not tonight," he interrupted. "No lectures on what I should have done or, even worse, your current feelings about 'us.' Baby, I'm dropping. I'll be home early tomorrow, before six. Everything will keep until then, right? Then, I promise, we'll sort things out."

"But the thing is, I can't go on as though everything is normal. There's never a right time for certain discussions. They have to pop out on their own, and—"

"Glynne, c'mon, please. We can leave everything in abeyance until tomorrow. I'll be home early. And we'll do all the talking you want then, I promise."

He placed an arm possessively around my shoulder. As we walked through the hall I glimpsed us in the mirror: a tired bread-winner leading his young wife to bed. Her hand, from habit, held onto his waist.

Still, I wondered, was I in love with Joe? Had I ever been in love at all? Was I even capable of falling in love? Now, as I had done many times before, I reflected on my "prophesy story."

Just a few months before I met Joe, I went out with a fellow called Leon. who had a good build and lazy brown eyes. I'd just turned seventeen. I wanted to sleep with him, but my Egyptian-Jewish parents had pounded it into me that girls who lose their virginity before marriage are "spoiled goods" and no decent man would want them.

So Leon and I found other ways to reach satisfaction. After one of our wilder sessions, he said, "I'm in love with you, Glynne. And you?" We were lying in the park on the grass, the moon on our faces.

I didn't think so. I loved his big hands all over me, but being in love was more than necking in the park with an attractive fellow on a summer evening. I knew very little about him other than that he liked me to lie on top of him so he could get armfuls of me.

"Do you love me?" he persisted.

"Well, you're dynamite, Leon, you really are. But no, I'm not in love with you."

He jumped to his feet and drove me home in silence. Outside my door, he gave me a look, his eyes smoldering. "Shall I tell you something you'll remember all your life?"

I thought, *Oh no! I wish you wouldn't!*

"You're doomed, Glynne. You're a woman who will never be able to fall in love. I swear to this on the head of my dead mother."

I put up a brave front and laughed. "Really? I didn't know you were a diviner." The word "diviner" just slipped from my tongue. I'd never used it before in my life.

But Leon's pronouncement stayed with me. And now I wondered if perhaps he had been right.

Chapter Three

The following evening, after a dinner of shepherd's pie with its mashed-potato topping baked to a golden crisp and chopped cabbage drenched in sweet butter, Joe and I faced each other in the living room. We'd agreed not to take phone calls. Cathy was asleep. My heart was thumping. Had I gone too far the previous night?

Joe fussed with his pipe until he got it lit and then tipped back his head to watch the smoke rise. "Look, Glynne," he began. "The things you said last evening . . . " He shook his head. "You sure can throw a fastball. Right to the you-know-where!" He made an imaginary punch to his groin, pulling a horrible face.

"I mean, I'm accustomed to your seesaw feelings—up to the moon for weeks, then *pow*, you suddenly crash, God only knows why, and next thing you're talking the 'do we really belong together' stuff. You say you need to make your own decisions, and then comes the trial separation bit, taking Cathy with you, too. Just about when I'm at the end of my tether, even reconsidering whether we really are right for each other, you, for no apparent reason, do a switch. You're affectionate, your eyes dance, you're happy. It all happens in a thrice. And I'm once again loved." He paused. "If I could fathom what the hell . . . "

His hand holding the pipe moved in a slow arc of bewilderment, the sentence hanging. I noted his 'in a thrice.' Both of us were keen on Shakespeare, and Joe would sprinkle his language with sayings from the Bard.

As for my ups and downs, I was well aware of them. My feelings could change fast. The same bawdy humor of his that made me giggle on some days made me yawn on others.

"Joe, it's not easy to explain. It's more than simply mood changes. I have a craving to test my potential. Am I capable of hacking it alone with Cathy? It has something to do with self-sufficiency, which I admire. I worry about becoming totally dependent on you."

Joe spoke coldly. "I don't want to hear it again. Let's be clear about one thing. No matter what you think you're searching for, I will *never* agree to a trial separation. Get it? I won't play poker with our lives."

"You don't—"

"Hang on, let me finish." His voice was louder than usual. "I will, however, agree to a divorce."

A slug of fear slid down my body.

"If that's what you want, I'll agree to it."

I felt winded. What exactly was I pushing against? I felt tears welling up. There were moments when he knew me better than I knew myself. And such a decent guy. Smart, caring, fun, and an inexhaustible lover. Sally had said that what made him special as a husband was how I was always uppermost in his mind. Once I'd raved to Joe about Charles Lamb, the English essayist and poet. A couple of days later, he'd thrust a dog-eared yet exquisite leather-bound book at me, saying, "It's not just for you, kiddo. Observe the title." It read *Everybody's Lamb*. We'd both laughed.

While living apart for a few months had seemed to me the best way to discover my own strengths and weaknesses, the idea of losing him forever was anathema. Just the word "divorce" gave me stomach cramps.

He continued, "I was pretty sure we were done with this moronic probing of our relationship, for a while, at least, but you hang on like a barnacle. Why? Do you think I don't know when you're happy? I see it when you're singing with Cathy, when we're together with friends, when we dance, when you're in my arms, when you read to me from your favorite authors. Also"—he glanced at the ceiling—"we do seem, um, more than compatible in bed. Do you agree?"

I did, and I nodded. I knew, too, in so many ways, that he was quite marvelous. He stayed cheerful even when he was flat-out tired, while I turned into a crosspatch. Of course he took on way too much on a regular basis: a ten-hour day job, teaching two nights a week, attending evening Party meetings, while unflaggingly arranging some sort of a social life for us.

"So, Glynne," he said calmly, "down to brass tacks. Tell me, yes or no. Do you really want a divorce? Or do you want to stay with me?"

As if attending a wedding ceremony, I heard the faraway voice of the bride's response, except the words came from my own two lips: "I do."

He nodded, almost matter-of-factly, then threw me a winning smile. "I'm glad. Looks like we're in for the long haul, kiddo. Still, you can't keep dumping your bad stuff on me, mmmmm?"

That odd habit, his voice gently rising at the end of that *mmmmm?*, unbeknownst to him, had often given me a sexual thrill. How does it happen that a lilt in a male voice can send heat up my thighs?

"Oh, dear. Why am I so changeable? I'm truly sorry."

Then his chin snapped up.

"You see," he said, "I had to make absolutely certain you loved me and meant to stay with me before I unfurled my plan."

"Golly!" I said. "Has your Johnson and Johnson stock gone up at last?" He owned twelve shares.

"No, nothing at all like that." He cleared his throat noisily. "Remember the early meeting I had yesterday? It lasted less than a half hour. Afterward, I just nipped off. No office and no Fink. I called in sick and played hooky the whole day."

"Oh, Joe! How very naughty of you!" I smiled approvingly.

He beamed. "My plan has nothing to do with money. I'm talking adventure. A few kinks still need ironing out but things look purty good."

The excitement in his face made him look even more handsome.

"And by the way, I'm never working in a law office again." He opened his arms wide. "Think new scenes, a new language, new faces, new cuisine, and new adventures."

"What, what? How?"

"In two months' time, you, Cathy, and I will be sailing for

France. We're all going to France for at least a year!"

"Please tell me this isn't one of your very worst jokes, Joe."

"It is definitely not. How could I joke about a thing like this?"

I began moaning joyous "*ooohs*" and shouting "I'm pinching myself!"

He watched me, his grin stretching his cheeks. "I'm a bit off the wall, too," he said. "Now let me give you the lowdown."

"Don't leave out anything. I want to hear every particle!"

"Well, we'll be staying mainly in Paris. I'll be taking my master's in philosophy at the Sorbonne, courtesy of the G.I. Bill. I can't wait to get started reading the Encyclopédists, d'Alembert, and Diderot. And you, Glynne, can study whatever you want—French literature or any of a dozen one-year programs for foreigners to choose from. As for our Cath, like her papa and mama—'son pere et sa mere'"—his accent was appallingly American, though he could read fluently—"she'll attend school, too, nursery school, with teachers called *mademoiselle* or *maîtresse*. Can't you see her belting out nursery rhymes in French?"

I leaped up. I wanted to dance with joy.

Joe's upheld hand stopped me. "Let me say something important first. I'm not blind as to what might happen in Paris. If, after living together abroad for a year, you're still talking separation, I won't contest it. I don't intend to spend the rest of my life with a woman who doesn't love me. Of course, I believe you do, right now."

"I do," I said, and I meant it.

"But if you want out, I'll return alone to New York. You'll have the choice then to stay on in Paris for up to a year, but no longer, before returning with Cathy to the U.S." He leaned back. "How does that sound?"

My head was tingling. It was wildly, gloriously unexpected. All of us going to Paris! I wanted to shout, clap my hands, run in circles like a puppy. And what a fantastic and generous arrangement he was offering me, too!

"Mind you," he said, "if we go to Paris, we're committed to each other. No silly talk of trial separations while we're there, got that?"

I nodded and kissed him on each cheek, then planted a third on his mouth. "Three is how the French do it."

Joe looked relieved. "To be honest, if you had insisted on that effing trial separation, I'd have scotched the whole deal. I needed to know we'd be together before telling you about it."

He stood up and held his hand over his heart. "*Allons enfants de la patrie, le jour de gloire est arrivé,*" he sang lustily, then stopped. "I must get to know more lines. You know 'La Marseillaise,' don't you?"

I nodded. "Our 'God Save the King' is such a tame anthem in comparison." I rose and sang: "'God save our gracious King, long live our noble King, God save the King.' That's what we sang when I was little. After every film, concert, or minor event, everyone would stand up and sing it. But what I really love is 'Le Chant des Partisons.' Part of it is so touching, it still makes me weepy: '*Ami, si tu tombes, un ami sort de l'ombre à ta place.*' Think of the Resistance fighting for freedom. 'Friend, if you fall, a friend will emerge from the shadows to take your place.' It sounds miles better in French. I learned it in school. Miss Einson, our Mademoiselle, a socialist in our swanky school!"

"Bravo, Glynne!" whooped my husband. "Promise to translate every word for me. You really are fantastic."

I rested my hands on his shoulders. "Oh, Lord! Will you forgive me for all the pain I've caused you?" I added quietly, "Maybe you shouldn't forgive me."

"Next time I may not." He sounded serious. "However, there's a small condition attached to this trip." His eyes bored into mine. "You're to promise me on your honor never—and never means not even one time—to bring up any sort of analysis pertinent to our relationship during our year in France."

Although this sounded simple, it would not be easy. Those analytical sessions he so hated were therapeutic for me. I'd always felt great relief after dumping my feelings on him. I thought that, as my partner, he needed to share my angst and uncertainties, even if he were their cause. For an entire year, when I felt doubts about our marriage, they would have to remain unvoiced.

"So?" He raised his brows.

"Right-ho." I placed my hand on my heart. "I promise on my

honor not to embark on any 'us' talks for a full year. I want to set out on our adventure with hope, with friendship, and with love for each other."

Joe raised an imaginary glass. "We'll drink a toast to that— soon."

He wrapped his arms around me. "To no more capers for a year."

"No more capers," I echoed, then added hopefully, "perhaps even forever."

"Don't get carried away, darling. One year at a time."

I now understood why he'd been in unusually good spirits the previous night for a man whose wife was half-thinking of leaving him. He'd had his plan. Last night now seemed far away.

"Joe, this venture of yours, it's staggeringly perfect. "

"Wait" he said, holding up his palm like a cop. "There's more." He inhaled noisily, making a familiar snort, normally irritating, but not today. "We're going to learn, all three of us, how to speak French. We'll live the way thousands of French students do. We'll get to know a different nation, with its values and its holidays. And, Glynne, just by being there, we'll be absorbing the French culture.

"And we must walk everywhere to really see Paris. I've always wanted to cross the Pont Nouveau—I saw a photo. Such wonderful carvings, and it was like no other bridge I'd ever seen."

"Well," I kept the snootiness out of my voice, "I'm going to cross all the *ancient* bridges in Paris as well."

He guffawed, "Hah! Fooled you. Pont Nouveau, or the New Bridge happens to be the oldest of all of Paris's bridges. The reason for its name? It was the first to be built across the Seine, so it was new at that time."

I was astonished. "Joe you're amazing !"

"You can be equally erudite." He groped in his back pocket, and held a thin booklet in front of me. "Picked it up free at the French Consulate's—absolutely crammed with amusing facts."

I took it.

His eyes locked with mine.

"But you haven't said how we can possibly afford it,"

"Well, we'll sublet this apartment. In fact, I have a renter already. Your uncle gave us a special low rate of a hundred-and-fifty bucks a month when we rented it from him. Our new renter will pay us two-fifty. So we're off to a good start. And the exchange of dollars to francs is sky high."

"What a gas!" I screamed. "Let's splurge on a smallish buying spree, a *petite* one, in France. We'll buy Cathy an elegant French dress. I'll get some gorgeous French hand-sewn underwear."

"Make sure it's low cut, black and lacy." He liked sexy nighties, but his skill in their fast removal was what often turned me on.

"I know how to live on the skimpiest of shoestrings," I said. "And we'll make lots of friends and eat at their houses."

"Actually, thanks to President Roosevelt and that good old G.I. Bill of Rights, my courses and books are paid for, as well as health insurance."

Although we knew several friends who'd been in the armed forces and had enrolled in American colleges, it had never occurred to us that one might go abroad.

I added, "We won't be like those tourists with cameras hanging round their necks, so busy snapping the sights that they miss the gestures and expressions that tell about the people. I intend not to take a single snapshot. The faces of our new friends, their smiles, the scenes, even the scents and sounds—they'll stay with us forever."

"And just think," he said, "of simply strolling along the banks of the Seine, and of holidays on the Côte d'Azur."

"And eating warm baguettes spread with sweet butter and strawberry *confiture*, or flaky croissants dipped in bowls of *café au lait* for breakfast?"

"Not bad so far, our trip *imaginaire*, eh?" Joe said. "Of course, everything won't be hunky-dory every second. But we'll gallop over the hurdles in our usual style." His eyes met mine. "And could it be, Glynnso, that our relationship might just benefit from a French—oops, I mean *fresh*—environment?"

He jumped up. "Something tells me it's the moment to break out the wine," he said, loping toward the hall closet. "What was your wonderful toast?"

Chapter Four

The day had arrived. It began like any other ordinary day.

While I got dressed, Joe was giving breakfast to Cathy in his usual style. "Oh please, Cathy, can I have one spoon, one tiny spoon of your egg?"

And Cathy's reply: "No." Then, relenting, "A very tiny spoon."

I smiled. Because it was far from an ordinary day.

A few hours later, we were walking to the pier where the ship was docked. Cathy, nearly three, sat astride Joe's shoulders, playing with his ears.

Joe and I simultaneously spotted our ship. Soon we could make out its name: "SS *Amsterdam*." Behind his spectacles, Joe's eyes gleamed. He threw me a look of delight.

Soon we were ushering an enclave of friends and family up the gangplank and into the large salon for a glass of champagne. My sister Sally whispered in my ear, "Glynne, promise not to do anything rash in Paris."

Our eyes held for a few moments. "I'll really try."

She shook her head, half smiling.

An ear-splitting *BOOM* stopped all conversations. Then came the announcement:

"All non-passengers must exit the ship immediately." Last-minute hugs, wishes, good-byes, and now the three of us were standing at the rail watching the crowd onshore get smaller and smaller as the ship glided farther and farther out to sea.

The previous day our two trunks—one packed with clothes, the other with canned vegetables, tomato sauce, ketchup, and sardines (because who knew what awful food awaited us in Paris)—had been picked up, and they were already waiting in our cabin.

We had decided on this ship because it was one of the few that took the sunny Mediterranean route that would land us in Cannes. It turned out we were the only passengers to be put ashore there; the others were headed for Italy.

In a small boat containing our vast trunks and suitcases, two brawny sailors rowed us from our huge steamship, temporarily docked in the gloriously blue waters, to the dock at Cannes.

We arrived at a charming small hotel, La Roche Fleuri, flowering vines of red bougainvillea pouring over its walls. We all stayed in one room, with Cathy's cot against a wall, where I nailed a large string bag so she could stand to reach her books, crayons and toys.

At the beginning, Joe and I were both dazzled by the heat, the charm, and the accent. Though our own French was poor, we loved to mimic the rolling *r*'s and extravagant arm gestures of the southerners.

During a six-week course at Le Cannet Universitaire (and Cathy with a babysitter each morning), we learned *la grammaire, l'histoire,* and *la poesie* and got a general idea of France. This turned out to be useful, because it told us how little we really knew.

Joe, of course, knew a lot about the French Revolution. We had argued about the guillotine. I said, "Poor things. For some, their only fault was that they were born rich."

Joe intoned, "In any progressive movement there will be things that are unbalanced." He easily forgave any revolutionary crimes.

Chapter Five

There were fifteen students in our program at the Sorbonne, "*L'école supérieur pour apprendre et enseigner le français à l'étranger.*" The name was risibly optimistic. Not only would the lucky students clutching certificates at the end of the year have a thorough grasp of French, but they could officially teach it to foreigners.

I climbed flights of worn wooden stairs and headed toward our classroom. At nine o'clock Mme Tourdzie would deliver one of her hideous *dictées*. Usually she'd read aloud passages from famous French writers. The first time she would enunciate the syllables of each word, turning her mouth acrobatically around them. Then she'd look out the window, taking in the scratchy music of our pens on paper, and repeat the sentence at a normal pace.

It seemed idiotic to me to spell out words without knowing their meaning, so one day after class I'd asked her, "What exactly is the point of these dictations?"

She replied enigmatically, half-smiling, "What is the point of anything, in the end?"

I had only two dresses (in France during the fifties, most students had only one). The one I was wearing today was a sporty wool, gray-and-white striped, that fell below my knees and was nipped in at the waist with a red belt. It had been sewn up for me inexpensively ages ago, but still it held a certain dash. But the reason I felt so alive today was my new shoes. Having worn only high heels after I'd turned seventeen, I had barely noticed how they'd hobbled my gait. Most young women in France and England wore heels, about three inches high. After arriving in the United States, my sister and I had clicked along in them even in our bathing suits, teetering along the boardwalks. We wore them because they made our legs appear longer. But now, in my new square-toed shoes, with low heels and soles of rubbery crepe, I could gallop like a pony. I'd claimed them just yesterday from a shop on boulevard Saint-Michel.

In these same shoes a few weeks later, I lightly bounced into the classroom. I returned Ned's smile from the far corner and heard blond Llona from Helsinki at the desk adjacent to mine say "Good morning, Gleen." In the rear, stocky Pyotr from Lisbon and handsome Hendrik from Delft were managing a conversation, gesturing amicably. The ice was thawing in our multilingual classroom.

As I squeezed into my desk, first turning my derriere into it and then swinging my legs elegantly around to the front (touted by women's magazines as the way to enter a car), I heard Mme Tourdzie's heels click as she marched in. On reaching the raised platform at the front of the room, she laid an armful of papers on the desk, placed her briefcase on the floor, and said, "*Bonjour Mesdemoiselles, Madame*"—a swift glance at me—"*et Messieurs.*" We chorused back, "*Bonjour Madame.*"

"Today we will not begin with the *dictée,*" she announced. With unaccustomed levity, she added in English, "I 'ope you are not disappointed by these news."

We clapped; somebody whistled. Words such as *"splendide"* and *"très bon"* filled the air.

"Enough!" Our teacher raised a small hand. "Calm down." But she couldn't hide a smile. "*Eh bien,*" she went on. "This is for the directors of the program."

She sat down at her desk and tugged an official-looking document from her briefcase. Rapidly she skimmed the top part, then raised her head.

"The first question is, 'are you satisfied with the program?' A few weeks have passed, and it is the last chance to have some of your money returned. So if you wish to leave, you may. Otherwise, you're in the program for the year."

She let that sink in before continuing. "Your knowledge of French at this point is . . . *lamentable.* In order to pass your exams you must work harder. The program becomes more difficult,

I promise you."

We didn't doubt her.

Bending forward with an air of complicity, she said, "Do you know that precisely half of last year's students failed the final examination? I'm sorry to say, they received no certificate." She seemed cheerful. "So are you sure you want to be here?"

Suddenly Ned got to his feet, nearly knocking his desk over in his haste.

Madame looked startled. "You are so sure you want to leave this class, Monsieur?"

"I'm going to get a glass of water," he replied, his accent very Yankee.

"You are obliged to take water before you come to class."

"Sorry," he said. "Be back in a second."

We students eyed one another, exchanging weak smiles, and pretending to think things over. Ned came back into the room.

Mme Tourdzie continued. "The second question: Why did you select this program?"

Pytror raised his hand. "To achieve a certificate for us to teach French in foreign lands was our course title, and that's why I'm here, to teach in my own country"

Llona said, "I hope to be able to read all of Proust's *Remembrance of Things Past* in the original. And to analyze it in French."

I wondered if she were serious. Llona, who couldn't get her tongue around two consecutive French words, hoped to be able to analyze Prousts's seven volumes by the end of a year? Ned's eyes met mine and he winked.

Ned announced he was taking the course after inheriting some old French cookbooks from his great-uncle containing recipes he'd like to understand

Now it was my turn. "I picked the course because French is a lingua franca, and so I can travel the world over and get to know different people."

"Monsieur 'edrik," Madame said. "We 'aven't heard from you. What made you choose this course?

Hedrik stood up. He had pink cheeks, a straightforward manner, and a solemn way of speaking. "For two reasons. First was to learn French. And second, I want to learn the language of love so that I can say things to my wife when we are alone."

The room went quiet. Hedrik was flustered, his English and Dutch ever more garbled. He was earnest. "You see, I am with my wife, Marieke, only a few months together, and I want to make my marriage better."

The silence was shattering. Then a small titter from the back was heard. That did it. Soon the whole class was laughing. We'd stop, then start again. We were not laughing at Hedrik, however. We applauded him. So much so that a few of us waited to take him out for coffee. He had been told by Madame to stay behind.

When he appeared and saw us, he grinned sheepishly. Ned and Pyotr grabbed his elbows, and Llona and I patted him on the back.

"But come on, what did she tell you?" we asked. "Did Madame provide you with some sexy love words?"

Hedrik blushed and looked up. "Two only. And I cannot reveal them." He shook his head shyly. "It is just for Marieka and me."

"Only two?" Pyotr's eyes were wide. "Even I know more than two."

"Yes, but she told me next time she will give me a few more," Hedrick replied. We cracked up, Hedrik laughing with us this time. There seemed to be a new camaraderie among us.

Walking toward Cathy's *maternelle* or nursery school, I recalled Hedrik's red cheeks and Mme Tourdzie's shock when he'd confessed the second part of why he'd wanted to learn French. I couldn't help smiling. I suspected he'd wanted to ask more from our bony-faced teacher, that he'd wanted to say, "If only I could whisper daring words and expressions of love to my Marieke, it would make our sex life more piquant and thrilling and make her love me more."

Still, his bashful wish had disarmed the dragon. Madame was gratified that the sounds of certain French words might unlock a lover's repression. Maybe even now she was compiling a list of lewd words for Hedrik, things she herself had not heard for many years. I was still smiling when I opened the school gate and Cathy jumped into my arms.

Chapter Six

Our small class was a kind of pocket United Nations. There was Hendrik from Holland, Pyotr from Portugal, Llona from Finland, Rita from Denmark, Giovanni from Italy, and Ned from Indiana, among others. Though not always a brilliant group, we were full of good will.

It was astonishing how any joke in French, no matter how feeble, sent the whole class reeling with merriment. We were bowled over by what we deemed Gallic wit. I still recall a tongue-twister given to us by M. Poivrot, our phonetics teacher, in whose class we learned to chant in unison, stifling a residual giggle: "*Poisson sans boisson est poison*"—"fish without drink is poison." Of course, it doesn't work in English, but in French it is *superbe*.

Mlle Cerise, a tall, stately woman who spoke with a small smile while pressing her palms together, led our current events class. She would read choice tidbits clipped from newspapers, her voice high with emotion, while we daydreamed and let the sounds flow over us. She would stop to ask, "*Avez-vous compris?*" Did we understand? We'd smile and make dubious sounds. "Ummm . . . partly. A little. " The previous day, when we'd replied in our usual fashion, she'd shaken her head on its lovely swan neck in frustration and said in English, "You are—what eez ze word I want? *Ouffe.*"

"Merciless?" Ned offered.

"Per'aps." She smiled broadly.

Part of the problem was that she'd start off reading to us slowly, lips pushed forward in an engaging pout, carefully mouthing a few words that were already comprehensible to us, like *absoluement* or *extraordinaire* or *évidemment*. But as soon as she got into the spirit of her story she'd forget us, pick up speed, and at times break off, panting with stifled bursts of merriment while nodding permission to us to join her in the fun. She'd be convulsed with laughter, throwing back her head, then abruptly stop to study our unsmiling faces. Then she'd say, "You have understood nothing, nothing at all." Which was the one statement we did understand.

We'd chat about Mlle Cerise later on and could gave a pretty good imitation of her pout and her laughter. Giovanni was especially funny, as he could thrust his lips out to reach his nose.

One day our favorite teacher, M. Poivrot, made an announcement. He had received permission for us to be received by La Grande Colette, the eminent French writer, in her apartment at the Palais-Royale. He said we were indeed privileged, for we'd be in the presence of a woman considered to be an emblem of the best of everything French. Her books, he told us, were read by not only by housewives, working people, and students, but also by France's most prestigious scholars and authors, like Marcel Proust, André Gide, and André Malroux. He explained that Colette was recognized by one name only, her maiden name, which happened also to be a given name. Her actual given name was Sidonie-Gabrielle Colette. He paused and made a gesture in which he simultaneously thrust out his chin and silently mouthed a wide *aah*, clearly meaning, "Don't blame me for saying this; that's the way it is." He continued, "She has now accumulated three more names, one for each of her husbands."

He said that he didn't feel it necessary to tell us to be respectful and considerate during our short visit. "Colette is now approaching eighty and is riddled with arthritis," he explained. Should we happen to address her, we must say "please": "*S'il vous plaît, Madame Colette*," and then ask the question. He really didn't want us to let him down.

He also explained that we might have trouble understanding her accent. "She is Burgundian, and even though she has lived in Paris for many years, she could never, ever be mistaken for a Parisian. In the small village where she grew up, Saint-Sauveur, now very famous, they bring the *r* from all the way back in the throat. For *rien* they say *rrrien* and for *trois* they say *trrrois*, and so on."

We tried out the new sound for *rrrrat* and *rrrrepondre* and *rrraisins* and any *r* word we could dig up. A cacophony of gargles and growls ensued until our professor held up a hand, suggesting we continue practicing at home. His final words were that we'd be in the presence of a woman who had achieved the rare status of being a legend in her own lifetime. Ah! How the French love to exaggerate, I thought, remembering how my concierge had said she had a "mad passion" for knitting. But M. Poivrot wasn't exaggerating, it turned out.

A few weeks later, on a drizzly morning in October, a dozen of us met near the rue de Beaujolais and the Palais-Royale. A gray pall hung over the streets and houses, but when we walked through the vestibule into Colette's apartment we felt as if we'd landed in a tropical zone. A wave of heat and light rose up to greet us, along with a stocky woman who smiled and said in a whisper, "*Ah! Les étudiants. Bonjour. Entrez.*" Her name was Pauline Tissandier. I learned afterward that she had been taken into service by Colette at the age of twelve, some forty years ago, and had become a devoted caretaker of her mistress.

Once we were inside, Pauline placed a finger to her lips and, via wavy gestures with her wrist, gave us to understand that today Madame was fatigued and suffering. "The pain in her legs has given her a night without sleep. Aah, you young ones. You don't know pain! One day—I hope not—perhaps you'll find out." Pauline shook her head in distress; her light eyes seemed watery.

For a few moments no one spoke. We didn't have a clue what to say. Then a middle-aged student from Luxembourg rallied, and in a deep baritone said, "*Quel dommage!*" Without knowing its exact meaning, we followed suit in a ragged, earnest chorus.

We already felt let down, having learned that M. Poivrot, sick with the flu, wouldn't be with us. We felt uneasy anticipating the verbal skirmishes that lay ahead, all by ourselves in the arena with Colette's rolling *r*'s and her provincial accent. Oh for the reliable M. Poivrot. Now it seemed we would be barging in on a sick woman who wanted to be left in peace. Pauline told us that we could stay with her mistress for ten, perhaps fifteen minutes at most. She studied her watch. She would inform us when it was time to leave. "*Venez. Suivez-moi, s'il vous plaît*"—"Come, follow me, please."

Quietly we followed her into a room only a few steps away. The walls were covered in red silk. Enhanced by bright lights, the result was a sunny glow. As to the surge of warmth we'd experienced on arriving, it was simply the result of plenty of heat being piped in. It was a minor miracle of sorts. This was a few years after the War, when goose-pimples and blue lips were quite the norm in Paris apartments.

Our first sight of Colette was of a broad back topped by a crown of frizzy, wood-colored hair. Propped up by pillows near a window, she lay on a divan. A table straddled it upon which were her tools: magnifying glass, barometer, a pot of fountain pens, a group of seaweed-colored paperweights. In front of her on the table lay a sheaf of blue paper. Later we observed that the top page was filled with her handwriting, with many insertions and heavy lines that scratched out unwanted words.

As we trooped in, she turned toward us with a smile. Her hand—fragile, still clutching her pen—beckoned us closer. Even before we'd arranged ourselves around her bed she was welcoming us, and at no time during our visit did she show any concession to pain. I stood with the other students in my class near her divan bed, close enough to savor something of her quiddity—her verve, her originality, her Gallic sensuality—but although I was drawn to her, she and I never exchanged a single word. Looking back at how I managed to muff such a rare opportunity nearly makes me weep.

Today I own several of her recordings, including one made in 1954, shortly before her death, where she is acting the role of Léa, the older woman loved by a young man in her 1920 novel *Chéri*. And while I still can't understand every word, the intensity of her voice stirs me. But when I heard it for the first time, its strength, its low-pitched assurance with those gravelly tones vibrating like a gong, almost took my breath away.

Here on her divan, she emanated an air of confidence, and in the thin, painted mouth and kohl-rimmed eyes I noted a dash of coquetry. I believe she was saying something about what a pleasure it was to make our acquaintances, but her accent made it difficult to know for sure. Looking back, I find it is hard to imagine how Colette could have been expected at this stage in her life to connect with a gaggle of inchoate students. But she did.

Two or three in our group bravely assayed questions, and she spoke slowly in response. I can still hear the high voice of the student from Luxembourg asking her what was the best time of day to write. After a short pause, she answered, "Whenever one is writing, without doubt that is the best time." Colette herself worked in a disciplined manner, and her time for writing was every afternoon. Her last husband, Maurice Goudeket, tells us that she wrote with a rug over her knees, scribbling away with a fountain pen for hours, stopping only to throw on another rug as evening drew near.

Liona, tall and blonde, asked what had most inspired Madame's writings. "Inspiration?" Colette repeated the word in French, her voice ascending to a high last syllable. *"Ah non, ah non ma jolie."* In a slow, guttural English she added, "Work. Work. Sometimes the work is hard." Then she lay back on her pillows, one hand raised delicately.

In the vast literature about Colette there are always allusions to her eyes, though no one seems quite sure about their color. There are references to her long, gray luminous gaze; the glance of slate-blue; eyes the greenest of green and eyes the color of rainwater. Julian Green, who visited her a year before her death, wrote, "They're the most beautiful eyes I know, as beautiful as those of an animal brimming with soul and sadness." Looking into them then, I saw them as tawny, feline, and touched with fierceness. I decided, too, that they were very French: they spoke volumes while revealing nothing.

Chapter Seven

Since arriving in Paris, we had been living with another family, Colin and Audrey Caldwell and their four-year-old son, Ginger, in Passy, in the chic 16th *arrondissement*. This excellent arrangement had been made through the Agency for Students' Lodging. We loved the neighborhood (which we could never have afforded without sharing a place), and we got on very well with the other family. Cathy and Ginger were playmates at once, and I was drawn to Audrey. Joe also liked her—perhaps a bit too much.

Two days after I met Colette, Joe rose early. Although I was awake, I did not stir in bed. It was Joe's day to go to the market, a dazzling event on Sundays, and only a ten-minute walk if you stepped briskly. He'd certainly hurry back, because after bowls of oatmeal and bananas for breakfast during the week, we all looked forward to a royal late breakfast on Sunday, or, as little Ginger named it, accidentally, "*le grand petit dejeuner.*"

As in many kitchens in Paris, ours lacked even the tiniest refrigerator. Thus, for us, as for most Parisians, food shopping was a daily occupation—a chore or a delight, depending on one's attitude, but in all events a necessity for all who liked meat, milk, eggs, and fish.

Once, on a cool night, I'd wrapped two pounds of stewing beef in wax paper and placed it carefully on the window ledge in our bedroom. Before going to sleep I checked it, chortling at my coup. "A free icebox," I boasted to Joe. When I looked for it the next day, it was gone, vanished into the blue. I hurtled downstairs in my robe, dashed about the shrubbery under the window, and saw to my chagrin bits of wax paper blowing on the yew trees, but no cubes of meat. "How could dogs reach the second floor?" I kept asking. None of us knew.

That evening on our promenade we met Raymond, our butcher, and told him about the mystery. He thought for a second and then nodded, declaring that it was not dogs, not even cats. He pointed his hand skyward. "It was," he said, *"les corbeaux"*—crows. Colin gave a bark of delight and shook with laughter, while Audrey, in her appalling accent, said that English crows didn't do that. "It is possible," said Raymond, "but in your country they do not have French meat!"

We all took turns doing the marketing, dragging along a tattered string bag that had come with the house. At times I went with Joe on his day, because for life and color, beauty and horror, scents and stir and bustle from every quarter and class, there was nothing to beat a Parisian market.

But today I wanted to talk to him, which couldn't be done in the bustle of the market. I was gripped by curiosity to know what his feelings were for Audrey. But what possible conversation could we have in a noisy market, with big decisions looming down on us, such as whether to buy a regular bunch of celery or splurge on an expensive celeriac. The latter, an ugly roundish root, had proved sensational when we'd had it grated and mayonnaised at one of the cheaper restaurants we patronized. Should we buy a tasty Camembert rather than the cheaper Reblochon? Or better yet should we take neither and instead take a chance on one of the fifty or more cheeses that had not yet touched our lips? I could hardly ask Joe if he fancied Audrey while dozens of vendors enjoined us to buy their tender eggplants, fine artichokes, crisp radishes, and even stringbeans without strings.

It wasn't quite eight, which meant I had a wonderful hour to while away before breakfast. Sunday was a lazy time. All but the shopper had a long lie-in: the kids could play with toys downstairs but knew they mustn't interrupt their parents. With a small stab, I recalled that when we'd last shopped together Joe had insisted on buying green olives for Audrey instead of the wrinkled black ones we usually bought. "She's crazy about jumbo green olives stuffed with pimentos but won't buy them—too dear," he'd said amiably. "Let's give her a treat, okay?"

I was about to ask, "And what about a treat for me?" Instead I said, "Okay." After all, a few olives wouldn't wreck us. As Colin said, "Since nothing fits in our budget, we're obliged to go out of it."

Now, in bed, I picked up my novel, Colette's *La Vagabonde*, from the night table. Published in 1910, its cover was torn and its pages crumbling and yellow. A very old bookseller at a stall on the Seine had dug it up. He'd given it to me saying, "Colette was lucky. She liked men and women."

"Oh, really," I said. How did he know that, I wondered. The price, thirty francs, was about ten cents. "*Parfait*," I'd said and for once didn't try to haggle.

The Vagabond is a marvelous study of a female consciousness awakening to the possibilities of independence. Its theme is whether a woman can love and be free. And with less than a third of it to go, I was keen to find out the answer. At the same time, I never wanted it to end. What I'd read about the bizarre way Colette had of forming longtime friendships with her husband's mistresses popped into my mind and made me consider. If I weren't jealous of Audrey, would I like her?

I thought about Audrey as I'd first seen her, when the small Caldwell herd had arrived from England one cold afternoon. Joe and Colin carried suitcases up and down, rearranging furniture and generally sorting things out, while Ginger and Cathy thumped up and down the staircase. Audrey and I sat opposite each other and talked, both of us ignoring our suitcases and the piles of clothes and shoes on the floor.

Audrey, in a beige woolen dress that made her small breasts look perky, her pale red hair brushing her collar, could pass for eighteen, I thought. But since I knew she'd recently received a degree in economics from Oxford, I wasn't surprised to find out that she was my age, twenty-five. She was the only child of a Presbyterian minister and a religious mother in Chester. Colin was a psychologist doing research on infant development.

At that first meeting, Audrey and I laughed until we were weak, so that once in a while she'd hold up a hand and beg "*pax*," just as Sally and I did. Then she told me a strange story.

"You must give me your opinion about this," she began. She'd been at the university library. It was warm, so she'd thrown off her scholar's black gown, unbuttoned her blouse, and begun to read.

"Then," she said, "a pellet of paper bounced onto my neck. I ignored it. The next minute another pellet landed on my bosom. I lifted it out and saw there was writing scribbled on it. Glynne, you'll never guess what it said."

"I've fallen passionately in love with you?"

"No. It said, 'You slut. If you'd like to know more about yourself, meet me at the quad in a half hour.'"

"Lord! How cheeky. Did you dare?"

"Of course. I found the whole thing rather exciting. Do you think there's anything wrong with me?"

"For enjoying being called a slut?"

"Partly. But more. I found this fellow Roger exciting. He never stopped insulting me. Somehow I felt relieved to hear all these rude and terrible things. You see, nobody ever had dreamed that I was anything but terribly intelligent and good-looking. I can't explain, but I felt the insults were merited. Ghastly, but hearing all the bad things I sometimes am was a relief."

"So did you go out with him?"

"Yes. Never tell dear Colin, for God's sake. Scout's honor!"

We shook hands on it.

"Actually," she continued, "Roger and I had a week together, barbarously stimulating, ghastly in a way, but I think I've got the desire to be demeaned out of my system. What do you think?"

I pondered the question. "Would it make you happy if it's gone?"

"Oh dear, breathlessly."

Then, as if I were an oracle, I spoke. "It's gone! You will never beg to be demeaned again."

"But who is to know what I'll desire next time?"

The green eyes under the dark lashes were hard to read. I shrugged.

Now, in my bed, I shook myself. It was time to get up and start preparations for our Sunday *grand petit dejeuner*. And while I was still jealous, it occurred to me that if Joe took up with Audrey, I might just keep her on as a friend. After all, she was fun. Especially when she wasn't looking too soulfully into my husband's eyes.

Chapter Eight

I was at the table gluing a porcelain doll's head back on its neck, and Joe, with his long legs stretched out, was lounging on our settee, talking to Audrey, in the chair opposite. He was high on his hobby horse about his hero Diderot, pointing out what a prodigy he was: a man whose satires and novels were as fascinating today as they had been when they were written a hundred fifty years ago.

I watched her watching his face. She was listening raptly; at times she laughed in her curious way that capered up the scale. Not once did I notice her eyes glazing over as I'm sure mine had during such discourses. Sometimes, in a gesture of sympathy at what he'd just said, she'd reach toward him, her thin fingers outstretched, saying, "Yes, yes. You've got it. That's it precisely." Or she'd throw back her head at the end of one of his sentences, her forefinger and thumb forming a circle, showing her total approval.

Joe tried to be matter-of-fact, but he could not conceal a beam of pleasure at her excited approval. With renewed confidence, he began to expound on another of Diderot's concepts, one, he said, which he'd found tough to grasp initially but was well worth the effort. He explained it, then said he wasn't sure he'd been clear. He scratched his ear and said, almost shyly, "I'd say it has really widened my own thinking."

Audrey spoke quietly. "You may not believe this, Joe, but I came up with a similar thought a few months back, but mine was, well, muddy. And no matter how hard I wrestled with it, something was missing." She looked at him, almost trembling. "And now you've turned up this concept again so that I understand it. You and Diderot, you've crystallized it so that it certainly will be a part of my own luggage from now on."

I nearly winced. Surely Joe must find her hideously effusive. I looked at him, hoping to see an amused expression in his eyes. But to the contrary, he was in full swing again, enthusing about an essay in which Diderot declared all ideas to be dependent on the five senses.

Later, alone with Joe, I asked him what he thought of Audrey. He answered almost flippantly, "Well, she laughs at my jokes. How bad can she be?"

"No, really, come on," I pressed.

"All right. She's swell. Anybody can see that—sensitive, highly intelligent. And—" he faked a leer "—not bad looking, either, even without makeup."

It was an understatement. Audrey was beautiful. Her green eyes were slanted like a cat's, and she had straight reddish blonde hair. An English rain-washed complexion went with it. She had told me that lipstick or rouge would ruin her particular allure, perhaps even make her look clownish.

One evening several weeks later, I arrived home from a late class tired, hoping to find dinner ready and everybody about. Instead I discovered Colin bumbling about the kitchen working on a spaghetti dish. "It won't be half as good as Audrey's," he promised cheerfully. I was silent. A spaghetti not even half as good as Audrey's awful Tomato Plat? I was not looking forward to dinner. Perhaps petulantly, I asked, "So where's Audrey? And Joe?"

"Oh, they went to the Monet exhibit."

"What?"

"You know, the new show."

"Yes, of course."

Joe knew exactly how much I had been looking forward to seeing this particular exhibit. Why had he taken Audrey?

I told Colin, "I think I'll have a little lie-down before dinner."

Chapter Nine

An hour later, in a sweat, I was awakened by what sounded like the frantic wingbeats of a large trapped insect, its buzz skittering me out of the horror of my nightmare. Often while dreaming I half-know it's a fantasy, and if it's a happy dream I can sometimes slip back into it after being awakened by some noise. In the same way I can usually end a frightening dream by snapping open my eyes. But this nightmare held me in its thrall. On awakening, I had a moment of disbelief at finding myself alive. I had been helplessly sinking in heaving quicksand.

In my dream, having taken pity on poor Audrey as she sank in the wet bog, her beautiful face distorted as she screeched for help, I reluctantly flung out my arms for her to grasp. I looked down and felt sickening terror: I couldn't see my legs. We were both of us sinking. We knew it was too late for us; we were sure to die. Then, strangely, our screams turned into loud insect noises. I wriggled my toes and opened my eyes. I knew I was in our bedroom in Passy because through the spindles of the mahogany bedstead I saw Joe's head over a newspaper. What joy to be alive, between warm sheets!

As for Audrey, she too was alive, and beautiful, and she'd soon be at the dinner table, where she would doubtlessly continue to flirt with my husband, right before my own eyes. I realized the truth of what Colette wrote in *La Vagabonde*: "You can get used to not eating, to pain in your teeth or stomach, you can even get used to the absence of a person you love, but you don't get used to jealousy."

The situation had all the trappings of a banal theatrical plot, I thought as I lay there in my marital bed. It went like this:

Act I:

Steady old Joe loves Glynne to distraction. Glynne takes him for granted and tends to walk all over him. She is smothered by his constancy, his repetitions, his tastes, and the predictability of his mind. The tonic she's aching for is freedom. She suggests a separation to discover her true feelings. He finds the idea abhorrent. He likes things as they are. The only thing wrong is her attitude. She needs to get back on track. Why is she searching for flaws in their wonderful marriage?

She thinks that fundamental things are wrong between them—intangible, sensitive, subtle things. Finally, she wears him down. Okay, enough, he says; if she insists on a separation, he'll return to New York in a few months. That's what she wants, isn't it? It will give her a chance to learn about self-sufficiency, independence, and all that jazz.

She agrees. It's a chance for her to keep her options open. Maybe after a few months' separation, she'll know if they belong together.

Act II:

Out of the blue, Joe is suddenly taken—taken in, perhaps—by Audrey, a femme fatale who wears no makeup. Glynne, amused at first, becomes cross, then worried. She boils into anger when she learns that good old Joe couldn't even wait for her to come home one evening so that they could attend the Monet exhibit, a show he knows Glynne was looking forward to seeing. He has taken Audrey instead. The tables have turned!

Glynne feels shaken. More and more, she can't stand the sight of Audrey. Glynne is even starting to have different feelings for Joe. How dare he do whatever he's doing with somebody else, even while he's never stopped telling her, Glynne, how much he loves her! So much for his dependability.

And Audrey? Miss Prim on the surface seems to harbor a hot passion for Glynne's husband. Oddly, poor old Colin, Audrey's chap, doesn't seem to care much. Is he used to his wife's infidelities? If only Audrey's parents would fall sick so that she has to catch a plane *tout de suite* back to England. By herself, of course. If only... .Oh dear, no! Take out the whiny cries. This is the moment when Glynne must become a prime mover of her life, resolved to do battle. *Ainsi soit-il* —So be it.

And so my mind ran on. When trying to cope with emotional matters, I often see myself in the third person in an attempt at objectivity.

What would Act III be like?

In spite of jealousy, I felt hunger pangs. The scent of tomatoes and garlic was wafting up through the floorboards. I looked at the alarm clock. Was it possible I had been in bed barely an hour? Sinking in the sands with Audrey, time had seemed to stretch forever.

I remembered how Joe and I had once talked about how puzzling it was that after a night of bizarre and unaccountable dreams, people awoke and easily returned to the world of reality. What became of all those dreams? I'd been impressed with Joe's notion that states of sleeping and waking were a continuation of life. One carries one's dreams into daily life and one's daily life into dreams.

I peered through half-closed lids to watch how Joe carefully fingered the newspaper, taking care as he turned the pages so as not to awaken me. Still, the paper rustled lightly, and it suddenly occurred to me that no insect had been trapped at all. Joe turning the pages was what I'd heard.

He would never knowingly rouse me, or anyone else, from sleep. It was against his principles. While deriding most forms of superstition, he and his five sisters and two brothers shared a mania about sleep. Not only was it sacred, but it was a source of everlasting interest to them, and one that permitted little levity.

From an early age their mother had been firm. A sleeper must only be disturbed in an emergency. At any rate, reading his paper quietly, Joe was unaware of his indiscretion. I wondered if he would consider dinnertime sufficiently urgent to awaken me. Then I realized, not a chance.

I remembered the first time I'd breakfasted with his family. I'd thought they were having me on. Now I know better. Joe's brother Sam, a big, tall guy who was both a lawyer and a pitcher for the St. Louis Cardinals, had sat down, beaming, at the table, before announcing, "Boy! I really slept last night. Total blotto! I mean it. I was out like a candle." He'd clapped his large hands.

His younger sister Adele had put down her spoon to ask with interest, "Really, Sam? Did it really last the whole night long?" She'd looked thoughtful. "You know, I would have thought you might have had a dream . . . ?"

"Nope." Sam vigorously shook his head. "No dreams, Adele. I tell you, I was out. O-U-T, bongo! That's why I feel like a million. I'm ready to . . . *POW!*" He took up a hard-boiled egg and pitched it to Joe, who effortlessly caught it.

Al, the youngest, at the head of the table, was shaking his head ruefully. "Jeez! You had all the luck, Sam. Last night was a mix. Off and on throughout." He made an up-and-down wavy gesture with his hand.

"Let's hope you were more asleep than awake, Ally," said Sophie, the oldest.

"More awake, sorry to say," Al answered, sounding remorseful.

"Did you have any luck, Rosie?" she asked, looking at a middle sister.

"How could I with my nose clogged up?" Rosie's voice sounded sharp. "You know I have a cold."

"Yeah, sorry," Al said.

"And how about you, Glynne?" Sam asked. He didn't want to leave me out of the conversation. I'd soon be his sister-in-law. "Did you sleep well?"

It seemed that everyone had stopped eating and all eyes were on me, waiting. I desperately tried to remember. Nothing came to mind except that I'd awakened one time on my single bed next to Adele's to use the bathroom. I said, "Fine, I slept fine, I think."

That did it. The reply set them all laughing.

"You mean to say you've forgotten how you slep-t?" Sophie asked, reverentially stretching the verb into two syllables with a heightened accent on the second. "Or did you have a nightmare that you don't want to talk about?"

Rose looked at me and tried to help. "For example, did you have to get up in the night for any reason?"

"Rose is referring to the bathroom," Adele explained.

At last I could be positive. I stammered, "Yes, I did, once, in the early morning!"

Everyone seemed relieved, and Sam nodded in an understanding way.

But Sophie was pursing her lips. "Are you quite sure, Glynne, you didn't leave your bed twice?" she asked directly.

"No. I mean, yes just the one time," I said, feeling worried, because now I wasn't sure.

"Well," Al said, "the question we all should be asking is, how long did it take you, after returning to your bed, to fall back asleep?"

"Five minutes, I'd say."

A ripple of disbelief passed around the table.

Then Rose said in a definitive way, "I'd summarize that Glynne didn't sleep like a baby, but she didn't have a bad night."

Memories of seven years ago. They made me smile. Now, with Joe watching over me, holding the paper up in his strong hands, I wanted his love to be as unquestioning as before. Had I already been supplanted in his affections by Audrey? Why couldn't he see through her? I'd have probably gone along with him if only this minute he'd said, "Glynne, I'm crazy about you. Let's forget about this dumb separation idea you keep bringing up."

But I was still dreaming of my independence and a life without Joe—at least some of the time. Why was I so changeable? I thought of George Formby, a stage and screen comedian from my part of England, who would end his act by tilting his head to one side and saying in his thick Lancashire accent, "Why? 'Cause folks is funny."

Chapter Ten

My eyes were still tightly shut as I thought about how I would act at dinner that night around the long table. Should I flirt with Colin to pique Audrey? Should I be aloof with her—she was somewhat aloof with me—in spite of her breathless giggles? Or should I be demonstrative with Joe, tickling his neck or pulling slowly on his earlobe? I'd never pulled his ear before, so instead of flirtatiously responding to it, he might simply look alarmed. That wouldn't do.

No sense thinking of what the lonely hearts columnists would offer in the way of help. There would be the old cop-out, "Just be yourself." As if one knew how to be oneself. Then I wondered what La Grande Colette would do if she were me. And it came back to me, what I'd read barely a week ago as I stood in a book-store thumbing through her most recent biography. She had a novel way of dealing with the mistresses of her first husband, Willy. She did not snub her rivals or insult them. What she did was forge friendships with them. And, it turned out, these friendships flowered and endured, enhancing her life, long after the men had upped and gone and were forgotten.

Was Colette using practical Gallic wisdom? I saw more in it than that. To me it had to do with her personal credo, her pride and quiddity. She would not stoop to hating perfectly charming women merely because her lecherous husband was infatuated with them. Despite the jealousy coiled tight inside me, I found her course of action admirable, and its potential reward was appealing. But I needed more time to achieve a cool, unemotional balance.

Joe, who had seasonal hay fever, suddenly gave an explosive sneeze. I opened my eyes and stretched, pretending to have just awakened.

"Hi, old thing," I said, in a low voice that was meant to sound husky.

"Glynne, I thought you'd never wake up. You were in a really deep sleep. I've rarely heard you snore before. What were you dreaming about?"

I shook my head. "Was I pulling faces?"

He thought for a moment. "I'd say drunk with happiness—or perhaps just drunk. You were boozing before dinner, I'm told." He made a comic leer. "Hey, Colin's on the ball tonight. Get a whiff of that tomato sauce! Beats grilled steak. Well, almost."

I inhaled. "Mmm, heaven."

"I'd have let you sleep on and gone down without you," he said. "Well, of course I'd have brought you up some bits and pieces," he added.

"*Quel* noble Joe." We exchanged faint smiles. "Well then," I said, trying to keep the huskiness in my voice. "How was the exhibition?"

He paused. "Thrilling. An exceptionally fine show. But we'd better get going," he said briskly. "We're all starving and it's late. We'll save the Monet show for dinner."

Thrilling indeed! Not his typical vernacular to describe an exhibition. Thrilling meant provocative, even wildly exciting. My mouth felt dry. I steeled myself for the dinner conversation, almost hearing Audrey's cool Oxford-accented tones ("We were quite bowled over by a little painting in the corner that had nothing whatever to do with waterlilies. Do you remember, Joe?")

Trying not to panic, I dressed, aiming for a casual, unrehearsed look: a soft crimson wool sweater (my only cashmere), a fitted tweed skirt, and black high-heeled shoes. The shoes would be a hit with little Cathy, who liked to hobble about the floor in them.

I could just hear Colin's tenor voice gleefully talking about his latest study as I reached the hallway. The babies—over a year old now—had been breast-fed and changed on demand, which meant whenever they fussed or cried. They were not ruled by outside schedules, and thus life was less stressful for them, Colin claimed. They would continue to be breast-fed until they weaned themselves naturally. "Yes," he answered Joe, "even if they reach five or six!"

Colin was excited about his work while mindful that the size of his group was modest—only thirty babies. He had weekly interviews with the mums and dads, tested the babies' reactions, observed the differences between his babies and a control group of those who were fed and changed on a schedule. The entire spectrum of the babies' behavior fascinated him.

Audrey suddenly interjected, "Of course, Colin's real reason for taking the job was so he could laze in bed until all hours every morning!"

She'd made that remark before, trying to be funny. Joe fielded it with a grin to Colin. "Can't think of a better reason!"

These studies were a first of their kind. Colin and his partner, Nicholas, kept track of the babies' behavioral patterns, emotional states, and test scores. Twenty years hence, the subjects, now young adults, could be compared with their peers who had been fed and changed by the clock, as my baby nurse had advised me to do with Cathy.

When I got downstairs I saw Cathy and Ginger in the drawing room deep in their games, making whirring and pounding noises and squatting oddly as they raced their cars over the map of our *arrondissement* Colin had sketched and colored, complete with stop signs, traffic lights, and traffic circles. The children raced their tiny cars up and down the roads, across bridges, and under arches, but never into the park. Colin had insisted that parks were for people only. I loved watching them.

"I'm a policeman," said Cathy.

"I'm a fireman," shrilled Ginger. "*Pa-pon pa-pon pa-pon.*"

"Listen," said Cathy. "I'm a policeman. So here's a ticket for speeding."

"I won't speed anymore," he said.

"Then give back your ticket," she ordered.

"No. I'll keep it for next time," he said.

"Okay, *ça va*," she said.

I swept them both into the dining room, where Colin, his tender face red from bending over the stove, was dishing out spaghetti into bowls, four big and two small. The evening proceeded without high drama. Audrey, sitting next to Joe, was shaking her head. "We simply can't agree, your husband and I, on which of the Monets was the most evocative." She smiled archly up at him.

"Ah well," I said. "*Vive la différence.*"

Hissing his s's in his sweet way, Ginger announced, "Noodlesh takes so long to eat."

Colin responded, "That's good. It gives you more time to enjoy them, Squire Ginger."

The boy opened his mouth wide to show his father the number of noodles still crammed in there. Colin looked away, but Audrey said sharply, "No, Ginger. Never do that. We're not interested in seeing your undigested food."

Then she turned to me. "Glynne, you should have come with us to the Monet exhibition. You would have adored it."

Colin said, "In fact we're going to see it, Glynne and I, next week, aren't we?" He smiled at me.

"It's a date." I smiled back.

"You and Joe are invited, too, if you want another go-round," Colin said graciously to his wife.

"Perhaps," she said, "but there's nothing like the first time. I mean, about doing anything. Joe and I were just saying how we always remember our 'firsts'—the first day of school, the first ice cream cone..." Her voice trailed off, but the game was already in orbit, with the kids offering their own "firsts": first kite, first movie, first yo-yo, first hoop, first licorice stick, first skipping rope. Then Ginger took us all by surprise by looking shyly at Cathy and lisping, "First kiss!"

Later, when Joe sauntered over to the kitchen to fetch the cheese, I saw his arm brush against Audrey's shoulder. She looked up at him knowingly. My stomach jumped. Had I really seen what I thought I saw?

Thank heavens it was my turn to put Cathy to bed. Joe was going off to a rally. "I'm not in a cheese mood," I said. "The spaghetti sauce was so filling." I grabbed Cathy's hand and left the room.

Joe didn't get home until after midnight. He'd gone to a meeting of union workers, held, appropriately, near the Place de la

Bastille, all the way on the other side of Paris. He'd waited in the metro station for an hour to catch a train home.

When I heard him step into the room I was in bed but not asleep. It wasn't his actual step I'd heard but the wheezing of our loose floorboards, since he would remove his shoes in the corridor when it was late. Most of the night I'd lain in bed writing a sort of morality play in my head.

There were two players, Joe and Glynne. Each had a major role, but only one was the star, and it wasn't Joe. Unlikely to be seen or heard by anyone ever, the play comprised a series of agile verbal sorties between us: dialogues of love and lust and forays into hate and reconciliation.

In them, Glynne always had the last word. She was, after all, the star. Even as Joe now prowled about in the darkness, removing clothes, I composed the last lines of the act.

Glynne, a smile hovering on her lips: "You'll grant that I know something about men. Mmmmm? You, Joe, were born with the misfortune of possessing gargantuan appetites for two things: food and sex. The former, unchecked, will make you fat. The latter is your downfall."

Another possibility was: "Joe, nothing's beyond belief. But you and Audrey as a couple?"

As Joe groped his way toward the bed, another line came to mind: "Let's face it, Joe. Right or wrong, it was I who first questioned our marriage. You've no right to horn in on my territory!"

Naturally, not hearing a single word of my dramas, Joe was totally happy to be home. After he'd climbed into our high bed, and until I dropped off, I was acutely aware of his presence. He arranged himself under the blankets. Then, like a cat positioning itself in familiar surroundings, he nestled himself around the curve of my back and almost immediately fell asleep.

Chapter Eleven

Colin was in the hall when we came back from the park, and Ginger rushed at him, crying, "Dad, we met a girl in the park and she let us play hit the hoop."

"Not hit. Roll the hoop, Ginger," said Cathy. She made a few circles with her arm.

"But you hit it with the stick," said Ginger.

Colin said, "Are you referring, by any chance, to that venerable diversion where children pursue a wooden wheel, whacking it with a stick every now and then to keep it going?"

They giggled, shouting, "Yes, yes, you know it is!"

Cathy said, "It looks easy, but . . . " She shook her head, frowning. "Colin, can you do it?"

Colin said "No," then took her hand. "Cathy, let me tell you something. In all the parks I've ever been in, in my whole life—and I've spent half of it, at least, playing, walking, and picnicking in parks—I've never, not even once, seen a grown-up rolling a hoop. And do you know why I think that is?" He paused. "It's just too hard for them to do."

Appeased, Cathy looked at him and smiled. "The girl who had the hoop knew how to do it. She rolled it round and round the grassy part. I wanted to have a turn so much. I was sure I'd do it like her, but when she let me try, the hoop went all over the place. It kept falling. I did it wrong." She scowled. "But Ginger," she implored "at the end, I did it for a bit, remember ? Didn't I?"

"Only for a little bit," said Ginger, stolidly truthful.

Cathy turned to me, her eyes shining. "But when I did, I felt like we were flying, me and the hoop. And *maman*—"

Ginger broke in. "Dad! I'm dying of thirst. Can I have some orange squash, please? We're dying for orange squash."

"How about letting me take care of these monkeys for a while?" Colin said to me, smiling. "I haven't seen much of them." He slung one under each arm, where he let them shriek a few moments before setting them down.

"They'd be thrilled," I said, and bit my tongue so as not to add, *and so would I.*

"Right-ho." Colin addressed the children. "It's orange squash for you—but only if you can tell me why you deserve it."

Without missing a beat, the children roared, "'Cause it's Sunday!"

Although Cathy laughed along with Ginger, she rolled her eyes at me, a sign that she considered such rituals were babyish but didn't want to spoil it for Ginger. Both of them knew how to answer all of Colin's questions that began with "Why do you deserve?" The right answer was simply knowing which day of the week it was. They deserved to go to the public swimming baths because it was Friday. They deserved cherry tarts because it was Thursday. Once Audrey had asked him, in exasperation, how long he planned to continue these questions. "Until they stop asking "What day is it today?" In exchange for these seemingly boring questions, he said, our kids would henceforth know which day of the week it was. Audrey had snorted, "Oh! And that's sure to get them on the inside track when they go to school!"

Now, as the three of them headed for the kitchen, the sound of Colin's buoyant voice could still be heard. "After you've guzzled your drinks, you must positively fly on the wings of Pegasus up to your rooms to lie down and rest. That is, if you want to go with Audrey and me to see the Guignol this afternoon in the Jardins du Luxumbourg."

Colin was so good-humored and original. He treated the children in such a natural way, and it worked brilliantly. Perhaps the key was that he believed in what he was saying to them. While he roughhoused and kidded, he managed never to talk down to them. He never stopped in mid-sentence to define esoteric words or unusual expressions when reading aloud. It was better, he said, that they try to understand rather than douse them with explanations. And so, I thought, while they probably didn't know who Pegasus was, it was perfectly clear to them that after drinking their orange squash, they must dash upstairs and go to sleep.

In the living room, Audrey was sitting with her newly washed hair fanning onto the back of the armchair. She looked like a gorgeous peacock. Half-laughing, she was looking down at Joe, who was sitting on the ottoman close to her. She was murmuring, "No, you mustn't, really. You must not, Joe. No!" She saw me and stopped.

Before I knew what I was saying, I asked in a sarcastic voice, "And what is it that Joe mustn't do?"

Joe looked at me with a silly smile, but his voice was calm. "Hi there, Glynne! I didn't hear you come home." My expression must have been stony, and he hurriedly went on, "Well, to answer your question, the thing I must not do is sleep with my mouth open in public, because apparently I make terrifying noises." He paused, and Audrey laughed. "Another thing—you've never noticed this, Glynne—involves spinach. I must not shove it to the side of my plate and then, when no one's looking, throw it in the garbage can. The kids will catch me out one day!" Again Audrey laughed, a silly trill.

I felt unnerved by this obvious pantomime but refused to let her see, so I said, "Well, I won't ever treat you to spinach again." God, I sounded just like a matron in a boys' prep school. So I quickly added, "Whatever would Popeye say to that?"

"Oh, something like 'I eat what I like and I like what I eat,'" Joe said. "But as a matter of fact, Glynne, there is one more thing I mustn't do—something important. Only I don't want to go into it right now. I'll tell you later."

"Fine," I said, as airily as I could, and managed a casual "See you" as I left.

The pieces of the puzzle were coming together. Joe, with his heavy streak of self-righteousness, was starting to feel queasy about his betrayal. He was ready to confess his trespass to me. Surely it was this, the thing he must never do again? Or had he and Audrey been battling about strategy? Probably he was determined to make a clean breast to me. Audrey's silken notes rang through my head. "No, you mustn't, really. You must not, Joe. No!" These words told me where she stood in the matter. The fact that she'd stopped talking when she saw me had given it away.

I flopped down on the bed. But in about two minutes I sat up. What in God's name was going on? I sensed that the tables had been turned. Soon I'd be confronted not by a doting husband but by one with an amorous agenda of his own—one in which there'd be no room for me. I had to take action; anything was better than replaying my horrible imaginings. But why had it taken me until now to see the obvious? No matter how hideous the results, I had to get to the truth. And not when he felt like it. I wanted to know now.

I opened the bedroom door and called down with all the authority I could muster, "Joe, could you come up please? Now."

I heard him coming up the stairs in his usual way, two at a time. He looked strained. "Is something up, darling?"

"Plenty," I snapped, trying to keep the anger out of my voice. "We need to talk. But not here. Let's go out to a café."

"Okay, sure." He looked grave, then said, "One thing first. This doesn't have anything to do with Cathy, does it?"

I shook my head no.

"She's such a swell kid," he said. "Sometimes, Glynne, watching you with her, you're like a couple of kids together, and—"

"Joe, this has nothing to do with Cathy. Are you ready to go?"

"Give me three minutes."

As I stood waiting, I felt downcast and sick to my stomach. Why couldn't he have at least attempted to be more discreet? The only word I could conjure up in my misery for his behavior was "indecent": such a bland word, yet it rose in me swirling red, circling my brain. It had been indecent of him to show me in a dozen ways how enamored he was of Audrey, how intimate they were. It was as if he wanted me to catch him red-handed. Was he getting back at me for the torment and uncertainty I'd created in him in the past?

When we went out it was raining, but neither of us wanted to turn back for umbrellas and raincoats.

Chapter Twelve

We walked side by side, a little apart, not talking much, while the rain fell and the wind blew in heavy gusts, so that we were soaked even before we reached the end of the short street. Joe grabbed my wet hand as we strode over the shiny cobblestones, letting it drop after we'd swung onto the wide boulevard with its line of dripping chestnut trees.

Two minutes later, as so often happens in Paris, the hard rain changed into sprinkles, and a pale sun was scudding through the clouds. All about us, tiny drops of water lay suspended. They were on the leaves, on the lamps overhead, and on the tips of balconies, while in the gutters the streams of rushing water were touched with shimmering gold. Paris swiftly recovers after a heavy rain, turning itself back into a heartbreakingly beautiful city.

But today I was unconscious of its allure. All my thoughts were on Joe and Audrey and the terror I'd soon be feeling when he would ruefully admit that he was desperately in love with Audrey and had in fact consummated their love many times over.

My heart seemed to thump in my ears, and I was conscious of the small, shallow breaths I was taking. I began to shiver.

"Come on, let's hurry, Glynne. You're going to catch cold." Joe took my arm and we began to run slowly. On reaching the café, we stood outside the door and, like shaggy dogs, shook our heads from side to side, flapped our jackets to and fro, and wiped the rain from our noses.

The salon was warm, and I was glad of the hubbub and the overfilled tables, mostly occupied by students like us. The buttery scent of brioches blending with strong coffee provided a familiar, albeit brief, comfort. At any rate, in a few minutes I'd know everything, and the suspense would be over. Even if he confirmed my worse suspicions, I'd decided not to let him see the hurt he was inflicting. Nor would I tell him that I might really love him after all. Of course, I knew that feelings heightened by jealousy should never be trusted. Anyway, no matter how bad the outcome, I was resolute about one thing: I'd try to act like my heroine, La Grande Colette. Were she to be compromised, she would certainly behave with dignity. Yet no matter how hard I tried, I knew I risked blowing it, perhaps making a hideous scene or, worse yet, a watery exhibition.

We took chairs opposite each other. It was the best way to talk. But suppose I'd been Audrey? Wouldn't he have insisted on sitting next to her, putting his arm around her shoulders? We ordered bowls of café au lait with croissants. Joe reached into his pocket and drew out his old briar pipe and shabby tobacco pouch. After tamping down the shag, he lit up and inhaled deeply, his eyes half-closed.

"Okay," he said, leaning back, blowing smoke rings and watching them rise. "Out with it. Shoot."

My mouth opened, but only one word came out. "I . . . I . . . ."

"Glynne, come on now, what's the matter?" His voice was gentle.

My head was heavy with words; they ran like schools of fishes swimming in circles in my head but wouldn't come out. I was saved from immediately answering by the waiter who'd arrived and placed two steaming bowls and a basket of croissants on the table, along with his jaunty, *"Bon appétit."*

Joe said *"Merci, Monsieu,"* and I offered him a wan smile.

We put our hands around the warm bowls of coffee and began to sip slowly.

After a few seconds Joe stopped drinking and looked at me. "Is it anything I've done? Tell me what it is!"

"Don't you have any idea what this is about?"

"Glynne, dear, just tell me. What is it? What's the terrible thing I've done?" Then he said, "Mmmmm?" It was composed of two notes, the second rising. It was a sound like a sleeping animal might make, a questing croon, and it was one my body recognized with a quick flick of pleasure. It was the involuntary sound he always made during our first stages of lovemaking.

Jealousy merged with desire. "Right-ho," I said. "Are you sleeping with Audrey?"

He didn't evade my eyes. "Would you mind if I were?"

His words knocked me off balance.

"I mean" he continued in a reasonable way, "you're the one who's always proposing a split-up."

"How long have you been sleeping together *in our house*?"

"What makes you think I'm having an affair with Audrey?"

"Everything. You're always downstairs with her. You're listening to her, and she's listening to you. You even exchange ideas in an intimate way. I feel as if I'm intruding when I enter the room when you two are talking. And Colin, if he ever stopped to analyze things, would probably feel the same. Then, when you just sailed off with her to see the Monet exhibition, when you knew I wanted to go and I assumed we'd see it together, that really started me wondering."

"Suppose you look at things from my side," Joe said. "I'm finally reaching the end of writing this very long paper, my master's thesis. I wake up with Diderot, I go to sleep with him, and during the day I think of what I'm going to write. This man sets me on fire with his brilliant, critical, inventive, and spirited mind. But when I read even a single paragraph of his dialogues to you, I feel your lack of interest.

"When I talk to Audrey, she's genuinely responsive and excited. I feel in certain ways that we've achieved an extraordinary kind of friendship, the kind that Epicurus touted, where minds actually meet. In Diderot you have everything—ethics, criticism, attitudes toward freedom, his stand on women—everything that interests you. Yet somehow you've bowed out. And yet otherwise, I think our minds are on the same wavelength."

"But Joe, you haven't given me a straight answer. Are you sleeping with Audrey or not?"

"Come on, Glynne. Hell no! Do you think I would deceive a friend like Colin? Anyway, I'm not in love with Audrey. Not even faintly. But I certainly appreciate her. She's a fine woman, and I derive a great deal from our talks. What's more, I look forward to having more talks with her, and—"

But I wasn't listening now. I was wildly happy, elated. I wanted to jump up and down, blow bugles, vault high poles, even dance a sexy tango. Instead I smiled weakly and through sudden tears said, "Oh God, Joe. I'm awfully glad."

"Any more things on the agenda, darling?" Joe asked. "If not, let's gitouttahere."

Chapter Thirteen

But there was more on the agenda. Although I'd been relieved to learn that Joe wasn't sleeping with Audrey, it took only a few more weeks for me to weary of him all over again. "Let's gitoutta-here" was just one of his many stock phrases that bored me silly. Without Joe around to confine me, how marvelous Paris might be!

Our first, trial year would soon conclude, and all I had to do was tell Joe what I felt. It would not be easy, and I didn't know how to begin. One night in October, I found my entrée.

He had just come home from a Party meeting and was in a state of indignation. One of the Party leaders had recently been missing meetings because his wife had just had twins. Joe couldn't understand it. "The man has no sense of priorities! What could be more important than the workers' revolution? How can he let his domestic situation make him numb to his duty to history?"

"Maybe some things *are* more important than history," I said from the bed.

"Nothing's more important than the revolution!"

"Really, Joe? What if you had to choose between the Party and me and Cathy? Which would you choose?"

He didn't even hesitate. "The Party."

My heart sank.

"Luckily," he said, "I don't have to choose. You support what I do, don't you? And I'm working for a better world for Cathy."

"Well, that's where we're different," I told him. "I could never sacrifice a person for an abstraction like history."

"We're different," he said. "You're not mature politically."

"And I don't ever want to be, if the Party takes priority over people!"

"Now, Glynne, don't get so emotional."

For I had leaped from the bed and was standing, facing him in my nightgown, tears in my eyes. "Joe, this isn't just some little thing. It's a core difference between us."

"We can live with it."

"No," I said. "I can't."

"What are you telling me?"

"Our deal was that we'd give our marriage a year in Paris. And if it didn't work out, you'd go home. Well, it's almost a year."

"And you didn't live up to your end of the deal!" he said. "You weren't supposed to bring up our marriage and all that nonsense for an entire year, yet every few months out it comes, all over again! Do you know how hard that is for me?"

"I just can't keep these things to myself."

"You have no discipline, no self-control!"

"Maybe not."

"But I love you anyway, Glynne." He reached for me, but I pushed him away.

"It's not working," I said. "Not for me."

"Here we go again," he said. "So you want a divorce?"

In the past, that word had terrified me, and I'd always retreated posthaste. Now I looked at him, unafraid. "Yes, Joe," I told him. "I want a divorce. I can't pretend I love you anymore."

Chapter Fourteen

We did pretend a bit more in front of Colin and Audrey, not wanting to entangle them in our misery quite yet. Then, late one damp night in early November, Colin received a telegram. He'd been humming a jaunty drinking song as he charted reading levels taken from his control group of London children, and I was deep in a Guy de Maupassant story. We were alone in the parlor when the doorbell rang.

"It's from the Foundation," he said. He tore open the envelope. First he was silent; then he moaned and slumped forward, his eyes shut. I knew that something terrible had happened. I'd never seen Colin like this. He was the one who could be counted on for balance and equanimity.

"Nicholas is dying," he said. "Cancer of the colon. He's got six months to live, if that." He continued, his voice barely audible. "Why in God's name didn't he tell me he was ill? In the last letter I had from him, the blighter had the cheek to tell me things were going swimmingly. Said his work in London was far easier without me there!"

I put my arms around his shoulders, then stroked his face until he calmed down.

After a while, he began to speak again. "I first met Nick fifteen years ago at Essex University. We were both doing child psychology. When I first spotted him, he was arguing heatedly with our idiot tutor. We got on well, Nick and me. We fired up one another. I couldn't believe my luck in meeting him, having him as a friend.

"After we'd taken our degrees, we began mapping out projects for England's poorest kids, schemes that would bring out their potential. We needed money, though. We applied everywhere and were rejected. Finally we did get a grant, and it was a generous one." He shook his head "Wouldn't you know it. Just when our ideas are proving themselves ... this! It was Nicholas who renewed my faith in people. He was so bloody clever and conceptual. An original. " He bit his lip and blinked. "I just can't bear to go on without him. Why didn't he let me know sooner about this illness? Jesus, why didn't he?" His voice choked. "In the last letter I had from him, the blighter had the cheek to tell me things were going swimmingly. Said his work in London was far easier without me there!"

I heard Colin out until we were both exhausted and he lifted his eyes—pink and tired— to meet mine.

"God! I'm an inconsiderate sod. Boring you like this ... "

"Oh, do shut up!"

"They want me back in London in two weeks. I'm sure Audrey, Ginger, and I can get away sooner than that."

"Colin, dear old Colin, I'm sorry. Miserable and sorry." I knew that for all of us things were changing forever.

Chapter Fifteen

It took Colin and Audrey three days to pack. A big brown trunk, two suitcases, and a large crate of Ginger's toys were stacked in the hallway. They were leaving the next morning. Two weeks after that, Joe, Cathy, and I would be moving to an apartment in the 4th *arrondissement*. A few weeks later, it would be good-bye to Paris for Joe. He would leave for New York, where he would look for a job. Of course, he'd be Cathy's father forever, but he'd be in the single mode again, and everything would be different.

He told me that he'd decided on a new definition of wealth: "True wealth is privilege—the privilege to be doing exactly what you want to do." He told me he would never practice law again. I thought he was right, and I was confirmed in my decision that we should get a divorce.

Within a few weeks, Cathy and I would be alone in Paris for another year. Even thinking about it was a challenge, and I found myself getting scared. I had to keep reminding myself that this was exactly what I'd wanted. But poor Cathy hadn't had much say in the matter.

The night before the Caldwells left we had a farewell dinner. The menu was written on a big index card with two decorations at the top: a house with a chimney that leaned at an angle, drawn by Cathy, and a long brown boot, drawn by Ginger. The names of the dishes were written in all different colors in the following order: artichokes with garlic butter, Glynne's crispy shepherd's pie, green salad, Comice pears with a ripe Camembert, and coffee with cream.

I could hear footsteps as Colin and Audrey briskly walked about, collecting their last bits of personal belongings, and I felt a stab of loneliness cut through me even before they'd left. A taxi would arrive at 6:15 in the morning to take them to the Gare du Nord for the train to Calais, where they'd take the ferry across the Channel to Dover.

Nearby in the kitchen, Joe absently gnawed at the knob of a crispy baguette with one hand while balancing a pile of dinner plates against his chest with the other. Cathy and Ginger played in the hallway, out of sight but within earshot, and I listened shamelessly to their chattering.

Cathy had on her schoolmarm voice. She liked playing school more than Ginger did, since she was invariably the teacher. "Remember what I said?"

"You said . . . " Ginger hesitated. "W-w-what did you say?" Little Ginger, always sensitive, had become more anxious by seeing his father's grief and had begun to stutter.

"I said you mustn't say '*bonjour*' in London, remember?"

"I know. B-b-but I can say *bonjour* to myself."

Cathy imitated Mlle Brisard, her teacher. "There was something else I said to remember. What was it, Ginger?"

"W-w-what? Tell me."

"You'll have to say 'hello'"—she coughed with the *h* sound—not ''*allo*.'"

"I know, 'cause I lived there before," he said.

"You'll have to say 'Good morning, teacher.'"

"G-g-good morning, your royal highness. I want some royal toast." His voice was buoyant.

Cathy's giggles merged with Ginger's before she shrieked, "I'll go and find the royal marmalade."

Then Cathy said, "Let's go upstairs and play with your journey map." A stampede of footsteps and a string of shrieks announced their departure.

The journey map was a large drawing Colin had made to help console his son. When he and Audrey had first told Ginger that they'd be returning to London, he had hung his head and wouldn't look at anyone. Audrey had put him on her lap and tried to comfort him. "Ginger-binger, listen to me. London's where you really live—where you and I and Daddy live. You remember, we came to

Paris for a year, and now the year is up."

He didn't reply.

"And," she went on, "you'll have lots of friends at school. You'll play cricket with a big bat, you'll get all the custard you can eat, and do you know what else?"

"What?" he asked reluctantly.

"You'll be able to hear Big Ben boom again. *Ding-dong ding-dong*," she sang as she stroked his head. "And if all that isn't enough, I'll bring you, my little ducky, to feed crusts of bread to all the other little duckies in St. James's Park. Now, what do you say to that?"

"It'll be nice, Mum." Ginger tried to smile.

But he'd really cheered up when Colin explained that they would have to take two taxis, two trains, and a ferryboat to get back home. Five different transports for one journey. Then Colin illustrated it by drawing the "journey map." It showed the rue de Passy, where we lived; the Gare du Nord, the railway station; the French town of Calais; the English Channel, with its high waves; Dover, in England, where the white cliffs are; and finally London. Ginger treasured his journey map and knew by heart each lap of the trip.

I was now placing the giant artichokes onto blue-rimmed plates. "Joe," I called, "it's ready. *La soupe est servie.* Get the troops out."

He roared up from the bottom of the stairway, "Din-dins everyone."

We'd had dinner together for months, yet of course this time was different. Every night there had been a fair amount of talk and laughter during the meal, kidding and telling stories. But tonight conversation didn't seem to roll at its usual pace. Still, the food disappeared in the usual way—fast. Audrey commented on how amazing it was that the children could wolf down such huge artichokes. And the children were remarkably efficient, as petal by petal they chewed, leaving behind the marks of their small teeth, until they reached the heart (the best part) and the choke (the worst). The hearts were cut up for them and they dipped the pieces into the garlic butter, uttering rapturous "num-nums." Next came the shepherd's pie, with golden-brown crests on top and a trickle of gravy. Everyone *oohed* and *aahed*.

Ginger asked politely, "Is this shepherd's pie?"

Audrey raised her brows. "You know it is. You've had it before."

"And you'd better remember it next time," Joe said, giving a pretend cuff to Ginger, who chortled and said, "Do it again. I hardly felt it."

And then Joe was off and running, telling a story about when he was a kid and had played a game called "Bravery" with Al, his kid brother. "I'd say to Al, 'You think you're pretty strong, right?' And Al would say, 'Yep.' So I'd say, 'Okay, does this hurt?'" Joe gestured with his hand. "I'd tap his arm very lightly. Al would say, 'Nope. I didn't feel a thing.' So I'd hit him just a tiny bit harder. 'No, nothing.' So I'd hit him harder and harder, until he got to where he had to bite his lip not to cry. Finally he'd say, 'Okay, stop Joe, stop. Maybe I'm not that strong.'"

The children were doubtful. Was Joe making up this story? Was he just kidding?

"Not at all," Joe answered. "If either of you urchins wants to play the game later, I'd be happy to play it with you."

"Yes, yes! Me first!" They squealed with delight.

After the first mouthful of crisp mashed potatoes and juicy meat, Audrey proclaimed it to be the food of the gods, adding, "I'll bet my best silk nightie no shepherd ever ate a pie like this."

"It's uncanny," I said, "how minced beef and spuds, each alone quite ordinary, when combined can be almost exotic."

"Well, I expect it was cooked with lamb when the shepherds first ate it. I mean, shepherds guard sheep, not cows."

"B-b-but daddy," Ginger said nervously. "Lambs are like babies to shepherds. They care f-f-for them. They wouldn't eat their babies."

Colin beamed at his son. "He's got a point."

"Good thinking, Ginger," we said and asked for a show of hands. We agreed solemnly that even the very first shepherds must have eaten pies made with beef.

When dinner was done, the children exchanged presents. Cathy gave Ginger a red engine filled with caramels. "It's two presents, you see. After you've eaten the sweets, you can play with it. And the wheels really turn."

Ginger took out two caramels. He gave one to Cathy and popped the other in his mouth. While chewing vigorously, he reached back on his chair and held out the small brown teddy bear he always slept with.

Cathy shook her head vigorously. "No, Ginger, you'll miss Teddy. You can give me something else."

Ginger continued to hold it out, but hung his head.

Colin's voice boomed out, "He wants you to have it, Cathy. Take it. Only he doesn't want you to call him Teddy. You're to call him Ginger."

Cathy took the bear and, looking directly into its button eyes, said, "You'd better be good with me, Ginger, and do what I tell you. If you do, I'll give you a surprise."

A smile hovered on Ginger's lips. "I think he wants a caramel."

Together they gently squashed a caramel against Teddy's wooly mouth.

After the children were asleep, the four of us sat around the table talking.

We said wonderful things we meant about how we'd merged almost into a family, how we'd brought out the best in each other, and how even with the children—or because of them—meals had been something special we'd all looked forward to. Audrey said that at times we were a radiant sextet, each performer casting a new light on another.

We drank three bottles of wine and became slushy and sentimental. As I looked across at Audrey's flushed face and shining eyes, all the grief she'd given me suddenly vanished. She had not, after all, won Joe's heart, so it was easy to forgive her. The fact was, I'd miss her: those flashes of brilliance from an enchantress who couldn't be boring if she tried. Colin, more than a little tipsy, looked lovingly around the table. "We have weathered each other and triumphed," he began in a pontifical voice. "I can't even imagine living without us all together."

Joe proposed a toast, but there wasn't any wine left. We cheered as we held up empty glasses. "Here's to us." Then, with hearts heavy, we groggily climbed the stairs and fell into bed.

It seemed only a couple of hours later that we were all in the hallway with the trunk and suitcases saying a last good-bye. I hugged Audrey, and she whispered in my ear, "I'll never forget all this. We'll be in touch with you all our lives."

"We will!" I cried fervently.

Joe bent over and kissed her on the lips. As he began to withdraw, Audrey, hussy to the last, pulled his head back hard to her mouth again for a final something to remember her by. He looked flushed and dazed when he raised his head.

Meanwhile, Colin had his arms around me. He kissed me first gently, then looked into my eyes. "How about one more for the road?" His mouth was on mine for a long time. Only when I couldn't catch my breath did he stop. "That's what I've wanted to do for a long time, Glynne," he said with a lopsided grin.

The doorbell rang. I grabbed Ginger and tried not to cry. "Be a good boy," I said, "and send me a card when you arrive."

"I will," he replied. He let me squeeze him for a few moments before he wriggled free. Then Cathy took his hand and they ran outside.

Last desperate good-byes were shouted: "We'll write"; "We'll have reunions"; "We'll throw a bash"; "You'll visit"; "We'll visit."

In fact, I saw Audrey only once after that.

Chapter Sixteen

A few weeks later, it was our turn to say adieu to the comfortable house we had lived in for nearly a year. We had been flabbergasted from the start to be there. What were we doing in this posh district, famous for its quiet, tree-lined streets and smartly dressed pedestrians who strolled along holding the jeweled leashes of esoteric pedigreed dogs whose names did not roll off the tongue like "scottie" or "spaniel"?

In all our time there, none of us had ever entered one of the designer shops that surrounded us. All six of us could have lived for twenty years on what an amber necklace in the window of the exquisite jeweler's studio might cost. We hadn't even thought of yearning for the camel couch with wood carvings from the nearby antique shop.

On the other hand, we'd often eyed the large cardboard cake boxes tied with ribbons held aloft or pressed to the chests of many of the passersby. And I, at any rate, got a fleeting flush of envy imagining the bliss of that first bite into a marzipan icing over some aromatic sponge cake filled with chestnut or mocha cream, moistened with a heavenly cordial. It was almost as dizzy a dream as the price of these gateaux.

For our birthdays we'd splurge on three tartlets: one filled with raspberries, one with chestnut cream, and one with a mix of coffee custard and bitter chocolate.These we shared with appreciative moans.

Our strict budget, despite the high exchange rate, was always a challenge. Still, as students, we were admitted free to all the museums and concerts, as well as to the National Theatre. Even at the cinema we paid only half price.

When we'd first arrived in Passy, we'd sit happily around the rosewood table in the dining room after dinner, speculating gratefully about why the Agency for Students' Lodgings had sent impoverished students like us to such a haven of bourgeois entitlement. And now we were leaving. Cathy waved her hand vigorously at Pom-Pom, our neighbor's cat, whose slit eyes always watched us from an upstairs window. Flinging back her head, she shouted up, "Pom-pom, we're going to miss you!" She stood staring up a few seconds longer, before following us toward the borrowed Citoën, a "*deux chevaux*." This was a car so small that Colin called it "*la portable*," since three guys could lift and carry it if necessary.

Before reaching the car, I felt a tug on my hand. "Do you think Pom-Pom will miss my stroking her?" Cathy was earnest. "I want her to. Cause I'm going to miss stroking her."

"Well, do you think Pom-Pom's smart for a cat?"

"Yes," Cathy said. "Remember how she pushes her head at me 'cause she wants to be petted?"

"True. So she will miss you, I'm sure. Cats seem to know who their friends are."

She nodded, satisfied, then quickly ran toward the car. Théo, a friend of Joe's, had borrowed it for the occasion, missing his morning classes at the School of Medicine to drive us and help carry our things up those four steep flights to our new digs. It was awfully good of him. He'd also been kind enough to look in on Cathy when she'd been ill. On one occasion he'd stayed on for dinner, and I'd suddenly felt his foot against mine under the table. Perhaps I left my own foot in place a few seconds too long, because ever since that night, Théo would cast ardent looks my way whenever Joe wasn't around.

Now we packed the little car, surprised by how much we owned. The fact was, we all got a kick out of buying secondhand things, and here they were, the lot: skis, pictures, a typewriter, jackets, dolls, candles, books. Abruptly I remembered how we'd applauded Audrey the time she'd said, "How can anybody *not* want to buy secondhand things rather than new ones? They're not only a fraction of the price, but they've passed the test of time. They work!"

Now Joe opened the car door and, eyeing the quantity of junk, grinned. "We may be poor, but we are people of property," he said grandly, pronouncing it "praperrty" in mock respect. He helped Cathy as she arranged herself over the books, pictures, bags of clothes, tennis racquets, roller skates, and a supersized bargain container of oatmeal. I turned to see my blue-eyed princess seated on shabby cases, holding tight to Ginger the teddy bear.

When we were all uncomfortably wedged in, the typewriter and winter coats heavy on my knees, Théo called out in his nasal voice, "Ready? We go. *En marche!*" He pushed a recalcitrant lever into first gear. The car shuddered and bounced, and despite the grinding noise, took off.

Soon Théo broke into song: "The Internationale." Joe and I chimed in. I had always wondered why the last line of the chorus of the British translation is "The Internationale *unites* the human race," whereas the original, French lyrics have "The international *will be* the human race." Was the change deliberate? Which version was stronger? I was pleased to have detected the word change.

Our new digs at 3 rue Malher looked like many other six-floor apartment houses in Paris built in the nineteenth century. Alas, it didn't resemble the white stone house in Passy. It wasn't as classy or as clean. Nor was the street as leafy, and nobody walked around in a state of sartorial chic. Instead, the inhabitants looked like us and dressed up only for special occasions.

The apartment consisted of a living room, a bedroom, and an alcove, where Cathy would sleep. We shared the kitchen and bathroom with our landlady, Mme Doucet. In French, *douce* means gentle or sweet. We found her to be cunning, a meddler, and a despot.

She hadn't exactly stolen our hearts when we'd first inspected the place. But our lease on the Passy house was expiring, and we desperately needed a place to live. In the fifties, apartments in Paris were scarce. Frequently, relatives of octogenarians or others considered not long for this world had a sporting chance of inheriting one, but they might be kept waiting for years. Even our previously reliable Student Agency's list of lodgings had dried up. They'd sent us scurrying excitedly to a couple of hotels that turned out to be ghastly. Finally, they gave us the address of an apartment on a ground floor. It was dark inside, and the walls were painted the darkest of browns. But the queer color did not camouflage the platoons of cockroaches on them.

Then, a miracle. A friend of a friend of Joe's let us know about three rooms in the 4th *arrondissement* for two hundred and twenty francs a month—about forty dollars. Not cheap, but do-able. We raced to see it. We climbed the four wooden flights to the third floor. (By now I knew that in France, the *rez-de-chauss-ée* was the ground floor, and one climbed a flight of stairs to the first floor.) I rang the bell. Joe looked at me, holding up his hand, fingers crossed. A woman of fifty-something opened the door and asked if we'd come about the apartment. "You see, it is in great demand," she said as she took us into the living room.

Joy! It had a coal stove at the back and a small balcony, too. And it was pleasant although shabby. I liked it instantly, even though I was somewhat distracted by Madame's hair, a dark-purple egg-plant shade, swept high on top of her head in snaky coils, like a Gorgon. She gestured for us to sit and then sat directly opposite us. Looking at me dubiously, she asked if I knew anything about *le nettoyage*." In vain, I racked my brains.

"I'm sorry, what did you say?" I kept my voice pleasant and full of bonhomie.

"*Le nettoyage! Net–toy–age!*" She barked out each syllable. She looked at me suspiciously, then, with a toss of impatience that made her waxy coils bounce, she rose and walked a few steps to a little round table. There, to our surprise, she spat hard on the polished walnut, after which she drew a handkerchief from her sleeve and started rubbing.

The penny dropped. Ah, cleaning! Though not too hygienic. What if everyone went about their *nettoyage* in that disgusting way? Before she tried any more of her pantomimes, I said, "Yes, of course I know how to clean." A slight exaggeration.

She gave me a shrewd look and after a pause said, "*Bon.*"

We followed her on what she called "*le grand tour.*" First, the bedroom. It was wallpapered with reddish frolicking deer oblivious to the crouching hunters with their bows and arrows. The wonderful thing for us was the little raised alcove off to one side, with a door, where Cathy could have her own small bedroom. But the bed that would be mine and Joe's seemed too narrow to be a double. Joe, too, was staring at it. Then, battling to be tactful, he asked, "Is this a double?"

"Monsieur, it is a bed for two persons," she replied quickly. "If you wish, I can get a tape measure from the kitchen."

"No, no, not necessary," we protested, not that we were convinced. In any event, Joe was scheduled to leave in a few weeks.

Mme Doucet thumped the chintz cover, remarking, "The mattress alone, just the mattress, cost me a small fortune."

"Did it?" Joe said politely. I kept silent.

Madame, still eyeing the mattress, said, leering, "I'm sure you both know how to fit in a bed—in the best way, *hein?*"

The tour continued. At the end of the corridor she stopped purposefully before a little doorway and flipped around to face us. Peering across her bosom, I saw a nice mahogany seat on the john. The dangling chain had a reassuring bauble at its tip. Praise the Lord that it wasn't one of the types where one plants one's feet upon two stone slabs and, following the flush, a Niagara Falls ensues, leaving you soaked up to your ankles.

"*Eh bien*, if you should live here, we must share this"—she pursed her lips roguishly—"petit salon. *Ça va?* All of us will use it together. What do you think?"

We simulated delight at the thought. Grinning like simians, we said, "*Oui, ah oui!*" at the heaven-made arrangement. Joe went a bit overboard with "*C'est parfait!*"

As the three of us stood crowded in the "*petit salon*," she explained house rule number one.

"For you, *les américains*, water costs nothing." She bit her thumbnail and flung it toward us, a Gallic gesture we now knew meant "given away." "But in Paris water costs a lot." Shaking her hand rapidly back and forth, she shouted, "It is a *formidable* expense, *for-mi-da-ble*—do you understand?" We nodded with a vigor to compensate for our disbelief. "And so you see we have a rule. In the W.C. in this house you may flush only for *les grands choses.*" She stretched out the word "*grands*" for effect. "As for *les petites choses, non, non, et non.*" She waggled a fat forefinger in front of her mouth. "*Jamais!* Understand?" We did. Never flush for peepee!

Stunned, we followed her, trembling with pent-up laughter, not daring to look at each another. Opening a nearby door, Madame said, "The bathroom, I don't need to tell you." Then why did you? I wanted to say. I seemed to be keeping up a silent dialogue with this woman. Looking at the squat galvanized steel tub, I was forever cured of a lifelong misapprehension regarding baths. A bath to me meant lying down, first on one's back, then on one's front, in very warm water, while frolicking with the soap and finally enjoying a long, languorous soak until one felt snug and warm all over.

Although the function of this angular tub, with its length barely larger than its depth, was for cleaning, it was more suitable for shampooing dogs, who couldn't escape over those steep sides. Good, too, for washing blankets and quilts. But for human delectation it was a disaster. There was room only for sitting, and each of us would be allowed only two turns a week. I wondered how the ample Mme Doucet managed to fit in it. And, more crucially, how she got out.

Next we were taken to see the kitchen. It was a typical inefficient Parisian kitchen of the era: a square, shallow sink; a three-ringed stove; a tiny oven; and an enameled table. Perhaps it was the challenge of overcoming such austere surroundings that had turned French women into such amazingly creative cooks. Here there were no pictures, no knickknacks, no homey touches to be found. But there was a small larder with shelves and a dusty window behind it wherein a handsome piece of ham sat next to a jar of Dijon mustard. I hadn't eaten in a while, and the ham looked inviting.

Back in the living room we each took the same seats we'd taken on arriving. Mme Doucet leaned forward in her chair and, smiling stiffly, said, "Well, is my little apartment according to your wishes?"

I nodded enthusiastically and Joe said, "*Beaucoup*, Madame." In order to check that the rent would indeed be two hundred and forty francs, Joe asked her what our rent would be.

Madame's eyes glinted. She pursed her lips for a few seconds, then said, "Well, with the electricity it will come to five hundred francs, Monsieur."

Our smiles froze; our hearts sank. Nobody said a word for several moments. Finally Joe said, "Michel Jacquemain, you know him, he told us it would be about two hundred and forty."

The chair itself seemed to jump as Madame shouted, "Non, non, et non! You must be dreaming. An apartment such as this for two hundred and forty francs a month? Not a chance." She knocked the table smartly with her knuckles, then shouted even louder. "But he's a crétin, Michel! He's mad, like his father!"

Joe looked at me, raised his brows, and expelled a loud breath. We couldn't possibly afford to pay five hundred francs a month. Joe rose and said wearily, "Okay, how about two hundred and sixty?"

Madame Doucet held out her squarish fingers to him. "Bon," she snapped. Two hundred and sixty. It's a deal."

We galloped down the stairs and away from her house on winged feet. We picked up Cathy at her nursery school and crossed over to the Right Bank, swinging her up high until she shrieked in fearful joy. We, too, were tipsy with success. An apartment in Paris. Quel coup! And within walking distance of the Seine, Notre-Dame, the old Jewish quarter, not to mention one of Paris's most beautiful bridges, the Pont Marie. We could scarcely believe our good fortune and took turns telling little Cathy the amusing parts of what had happened at Mme Doucet's. She threw her head back giggling, her blond hair flying, delighted to be included in all the fun.

Chapter Seventeen

The apartment wasn't like our Passy place, but it wasn't at all bad. It was bright, there were no bad smells or weird noises, and our bedroom had a charming balcony that was sunny at midday. Best of all, we could walk to almost anywhere on the Left Bank. The sight of the Seine, the little parks, the statues, the old churches evoked a thrilling nostalgia for something we'd never actually seen. One could walk along the quai and cross halfway on the Pont Neuf to the Île de la Cité, and *voilà*, the world-famous cathedral Notre-Dame.

I could also walk to the Sorbonne. The walk took me only a few more minutes than taking the metro. Fifteen minutes in a different direction led to another wonderful surprise, the Place des Vosges, a beautiful three-hundred-year-old square with a sandpit where Cathy could dig to her heart's content and I could sit back on one of the elegant wrought-iron benches and look at the surrounding buildings, all architectural gems.

The minus side of our new digs was having to share the kitchen with our pathological landlady, who lived in a semi-permanent state of reproach. It took the form of aggrieved questions, such as "Where did you put my asparagus dish?" or "Do you and your family remember what I told you about the toilet, *hein*?" or "I trust you're not taking more than the allotted two baths a week." She always added, "No more than two, but *less* if you prefer." Her lips might twitch at her joke.

Joe's advice was to ignore her or josh her out of it. "But if I ignore her she's likely to hit me, and if I kid her she thinks I'm laughing at her. The one way to calm her down is with an apology."

"Well, give her one now and then," he said.

Actually, with only three weeks before Joe left for New York, I was in need of a little calming myself. As his time in Paris grew shorter, Joe became quieter. But oddly, the strain of our impending separation never seemed to diminish his physical desire and pleasure. I attributed this to the fact that his parents came from the Mideast, as did mine. I was brought up to think that Egyptians possessed seeds as rich and fertile as the Nile.

Afterwards, sleepy yet with my mind agitated, guilt would rise up in me like an earthworm after a storm. What did I think I was doing? Why was I doing such good things with a man I wanted to leave? I would wake up in the early hours of the morning and lie listening to the rhythm of his breathing. At such times he seemed impenetrable, in a private world never to be revealed, and I'd want to reach over and touch him. I felt sick at heart making such a mess of our marriage.

Even more, I craved the impossible: reassurance from him, the very one from whom I was planning to escape. I wanted to hear him say that he understood why I wanted him gone; that this was the precisely the right time for me to try living alone; even to wish me luck in achieving my new independence. I wanted him to say that on balance I was doing something that needed to be done, even to say, "You'll be back on track, back on your feet, after a short time."

Was I being self-indulgent? Irresponsible? Egotistical? Possibly all three. I'm sure our friends thought so. They respected Joe immensely and saw us as an ideal couple, one who should grow old together like mushrooms on a hillside. How could I, for no tangible reason, shatter such a harmonious picture?

Some of our friends concluded that I'd got myself a lover. A student from Senegal, a good friend of mine, asked me up to her room for tea, determined to save my marriage. While were talking, she'd abruptly said, "Would you mind if I give you a bit of advice, Glynne? I say it because you are dear to me."

"You may. But please, not too much."

She smiled. "Small infatuations happen sometimes, but they pass over like a sandstorm. Joe is forever. He will cherish you always. He is your husband. And he belongs to you."

She was astonished when I told her that there was no other man in my life. I explained to her that when Joe and I were with other people, we hit it off. We seemed happy. Joe, tall, humorous, genial, politically far left; me, slim, mercurial, quick to laugh or cry. Like a comedy team. We could top each other's stories, making them better and funnier. Our serious times revolved around politics and fighting for a better world. We discussed the unity of the French workers compared with working people in the States. He knew a great deal and was generous about sharing it.

I'd gotten used to his habits of almost never talking about the lives of our friends: their characters, their idiosyncrasies, what we liked or disliked about them. He rarely spoke of his past lovers and wasn't interested in mine. We never, ever spoke of that time he'd learned I'd had a brief affair on a short trip to London a few years ago.

I'd gone to see my brother and came home by ship. Onboard, I'd met an irresistible Scotsman. We'd had a magical time. Just before leaving the boat, he'd asked me if I would contemplate leaving my husband.

That night in bed, with Joe's arms around me, he whispered, "Darling! You look so smashing. Did you make any conquests? How could you not?"

"Well,... " I shook my head. Better not tell.

He persisted. "It's only natural that you would. Glynne, and it's fine with me. I can understand. Things sometimes just happen."

He'd been warm and persuasive, so I said, "Actually, there was one, very briefly."

"It's okay with me. You mean you slept with him once?"

"Yes," I confessed. "It had nothing to do with love."

"Just that one time?" he asked.

"Twice," I said.

Then, without warning, he'd leaped out of bed, dragging one of the blankets with him, and marched off into the living room. I was stunned.

"But you said you understood, that it was natural, that you

weren't mad," I babbled at his retreating back.

He slept by himself on the living room couch for a week. Then, one night as I was reading in bed, he appeared naked and resumed sleeping in our big bed.

Chapter Eighteen

Each morning I went to the Sorbonne as though I were another ordinary carefree student, clattering up the wide stone steps of this ancient building. But the knowledge of Joe's departure in just a week would make my insides pulse with terror.

Once I reached the classroom and wedged myself into the musty oak desk, the fear abated. Alongside my classmates, I felt calmer. The slanted desktop with its empty inkwell in the corner was a crisscross of scratches and indentations in which here and there a letter or part of a word could be construed. Those four letters near the top spelled *bête*, meaning stupid. French children say it all the time to each another, and parents admonish their children's silly questions with "*Ne sois pas bête*"—"Don't be silly."

Several lopped-off letters covered with scribbles smeared with brown varnish were above "bête." I looked at them often but could never discover who was *bete*. It could be Anne or Allan, unless the A was actually F. In that case the dunce could be Farou or Francois.

What a comfort it was to be sitting at this old desk impregnated with secrets. And here I was destroying a marriage meant for a lifetime. But why think about it? The die was cast, wasn't it? Not irrevocably. At any time before Joe left I had only to grab him and say what a fool I'd been, how much I needed him, and we'd be a couple again. Only last night I might have held out an olive branch to him.

We were lying on our backs in the four-poster with the light off, wide awake, each waiting for the other to speak. I half wanted to initiate one of our heavy "us" talks but knew better. I searched for something easy to say that didn't sound forced. Ah, of course, the milk! In the fifties there was only one kind of milk in Paris. It was full-fat and unhomogenized, so that each liter bottle showed a two-inch head of cream on top.

"Joe," I said, "when the concierge brought up the milk today, after you'd left for class, it was like yesterday's, really watery. She must be nicking the cream off the top. Because I'm not French, perhaps she thinks I won't notice."

"Well, it's not necessarily our concierge," he replied. "Mlle Brun's a pretty good egg. It could be Mme Doucet. She's got more than a touch of larceny in her. Old Mlle Brun may be grumpy, and who wouldn't be if your sleep was interrupted all night by people entering and leaving?"

"Yes, but what can I do about the milk?"

"We're never likely to find out who steals our cream. But if it is Mme Doucet, her crime will be her punishment. Her *avoirdupois* will keep going up!"

"But Joe, we're left drinking pale-blue milk while she licks her creamy chops." I added, "Hey, how about an indirect approach? You could say, "Madame, we were wondering, my wife and I, if in Paris one needs a special coupon to buy milk without cream. And is it cheaper?"

"No, I could not say that. Nor could you. She'd be insulted, or pretend to be. Either drink watery milk or go and buy your own. And now, for God's sake, stop worrying about it." He touched my shoulder. "Heavens! You're freezing." He drew me close with a muscled arm. I knew where this was leading and responded not merely from long habit, nor acquiescence, but from my own pent-up lust, as powerful as his.

Afterwards, it took me a long time to fall asleep. For months I had not felt so at one with him. It had been tumultuous—revelations, tears, laughter, passion. Had he at that moment uttered endearments rather than falling asleep, I might have snatched at an olive branch. Perhaps another year together?

At the Sorbonne, sheltered behind ancient walls, it was a relief to escape from incessant thoughts about Joe's departure and Cathy's reactions. How could I think up ways to distract her that would cost no money?

A practical doubt also dug its way into my mind. Could I actually manage on the small amount of money Joe would be sending? I'd rarely spent more than thirty dollars at a time, and suddenly my job description would be financial director. Budgeting wasn't so hard if one had enough to budget with. Did I? And another matter: I'd better develop a better relationship with Mme Doucet. Cathy and I had to find a way to live happily in her house without being bullied or having our milk skimmed for us. And without spending precious time with her.

As the clock struck nine, Mme Tourdzie entered the classroom. Today's class was on Marcel Proust. She began by expressing disdain at the English translation of his novel's title, *Remembrance of Things Past*. "*À La Recherche du Temps Perdu* signifies a search for times long forgotten. It is active. The English is passive."

In spite of Proust's labyrinthine sentences, with their long subordinate clauses, each explaining or modifying the previous one, his work was not hard to read, according to Mme Tourdzie. And she was right. It just took a long time. For me, Proust's discovery that "involuntary memories"—sounds, smells, sights, tastes that leap to mind suddenly without forethought—are more powerful than those deliberately dredged up seemed not only true but fascinating.

As for his tale of the *madeleine*, the little sponge cake the child Marcel dipped in his herbal tea at his grandmother's house in Combray, Mme Tourdzie's lively telling of the well-known story was beautiful. The class was excited along with her. It was a wondrous notion that when Marcel was older it took but a few sips of this same tea and a nibble of a *madeleine* to again relive the colorful universe of his childhood. Madame herself was transformed as she read to us, first in French, then in terrible English. Soon her gray eyes shone, her cheeks turned pink, and her voice quivered with excitement. She won us over entirely. Her enthusiasm not only made us like her, but it egged us on to read page after page of what she considered the most important book ever written.

Five days before Joe was to go back to New York, he and I went to see a film with my favorite French actor, Jean Gabin, who was the toast of Paris at the time. Handsome and craggy, he had starred in such legendary films as *La Grande Illusion* and *La Bête Humaine*. Now in his forties, he still smoldered onscreen. As Joe and I walked home, we succeeded in being quite merry. When we got back to the apartment, Joe, with an air of conspiracy, said he had something to tell me.

After he'd made us two mugs of hot chocolate, we sat sipping across the table. He took a breath and slowly shook his head.

"I know you're going to overreact, Glynne, but after some heavy soul-searching, I've changed my mind about our separating."

Something crawled in the pit of my stomach.

"In all good faith, Glynne darling, I can't let you live alone with Cathy in Paris. I don't think you could manage."

"After all the agony of these weeks, all the things we've hashed and rehashed. now this?" My voice was shrill in my ears. My breath was fast. But I wasn't indecisive.

"Calm down, Glynne. Hear me out. Try, just try, to be objective. Take punctuality—"

"You take it!"

"You're almost never on time. Even for parties you're dying to go to. You've never been early in your life for anything. How can you be when you leave the house at the time you should be there? I know you'll be late getting Cathy to school—with a different, breathless reason each time. Maybe," he said, only half-kidding, "you'll even forget to bring her home. You did that once, remember?"

It was true. I'd left Cathy in her carriage outside the A&P when she was four weeks old. My friend Nina was with me, and we were laughing about something when we came out of the store. Walking home to the apartment, we were totally immersed in conversation until I froze, realizing that Cathy wasn't with us.

In my defense, it was the first time I'd taken my baby out, since up until then the nurse had taken her for walks. When Nina and I retrieved her outside the A&P, Cathy was sound asleep.

Joe had laughed at this four years ago. Well, he'd smiled. How dare he throw it at me now?

"If you think I'm going to sit here while you bring up everything I've ever done wrong—"

"Even French. We've been here almost a year and you've not learned much. You don't take things seriously. I'm not blaming you for that, it's your nature, but—"

"How would you know what I've learned? It isn't as though we ever talk together in French. And with your accent . . . Joe, please!"

"Well, Glynne, I'm responsible for you and Cathy. And I happen to care for you as well."

"Oh, don't! Joe, I don't want to be so cared for right now. You remember how I always poo-pooed people trying to find their identities? Well, I'm one of them now. I must find out what I'm capable of. Oh Lord, haven't we covered everything a hundred times already?"

Joe blew out a long breath. "You've got things wrong. Listen, Glynne, you've got all the qualities a guy could want, and you're my gal. The thing you don't get is obvious. You need me."

"I don't want—"

"Just listen. If, in a couple of months, when we're back in New York, you want to go your own way, then I'll do all I can to help you. How about that?"

"No. I'm not going back with you to New York."

As though he hadn't heard me, he calmly continued. "There's room for you on my flight. I've checked. But you'll have to start packing early in the morning. It's too late tonight. I'll take care of everything else.

"Joe, I'm *not* going back with you. Really!"

"Stop screaming, you'll wake Cathy," he admonished in virtuously low tones.

"Joe," I said, trying to sound calm. "The whole point is that I don't want you to take care of my life, even if it is easier for me. I need to take care of myself and Cathy for a while, even if I make mistakes. I'm not a slow learner. Maybe the reason we've stayed together this long is because you make it so easy. It's your friends, your meetings, your plans, your vacations, even your opinions— it's a comfortable sock to slip into. But I really need the chance to move into my own life." I stopped. I'd forgotten to bring up something. "Tell me, what happened to your support for women's rights?"

"C'mon! I'm a hundred percent behind them. Equal pay, equal status—the lot."

"You support women's rights?" I said slowly. "You support *other* women's rights."

He swerved onto a new track. "You don't know the meaning of organization. You come and go, you laugh and cry, you do whatever the spirit moves you to—you're such a kid. So in the last analysis, I'm concerned about Cathy, and I don't want to leave her with you."

I reminded him of his solemn promise of a year ago, before we left for Paris. How he'd said that if after a year together in Paris I still wanted to separate, he'd agree. He didn't deny it. He bit his lip. And I told him that maybe I did love him—who knew, after all, what love was?—but that it would take a team of horses to get me to leave Paris right now.

It was nearly three in the morning when he finally capitulated. Stonily. The light had gone from his face. I felt ashamed by his expression, but at the same time a surge of relief swept over me.

He told me he could afford only a meager sum for Cathy and me to live on. He'd send me a hundred and thirty dollars on the first day of each month. This money would be taken from the rent he obtained from subletting our apartment. I would have to spend it very carefully.

"We'll manage," I said. "Remember my thrifty meals. Breaded meat loaf, shepherd's pie, pot-au-feu, and squash stuffed with rice. Cheap and good."

"I've never complained about your cooking, Glynne. It's better than my mother's!" This was an old joke, since his mother was a hopeless cook. "My only complaint is you dirty a dozen plates just for the two of us. And I'm the dishwasher!" He managed a wan smile.

We were both exhausted.

"C'mon, Glynne," he said. "Let's get to bed. We've got to get up today—soon."

On the dull Paris morning that Joe left, the three of us stood, hand in hand, on the street in front of our house on rue Malher waiting for the taxi that would take Joe to the airport. His overstuffed suitcase—filled mostly with books—stood nearby on the pavement. When the taxi arrived, Cathy let out a howl. I felt tears in my eyes. I noticed that Joe's eyes seemed bleary behind his spectacles.

Still he kidded with Cathy. "Hey you!" He held her up high so that they faced each other. "Guess what I'll do first, Cath, the very second I reach New York?"

She brushed her eyes with the back of her hand. Her chin trembled. Her voice was a reedy flute. "You'll m-m-make a cup of coffee." She was trying not to cry.

"Aha! Wrong. That will be the second thing."

The driver banged the trunk shut.

"What, then?" she said dully.

"Well, the first thing—the very first, not the second or the third—is I'll sit down and write a letter to you. Will you answer me?"

She looked anxious. "B-b-but Daddy, I don't know how to spell!"

"Well, you'll tell Mummy things to tell me. Things you're thinking and whatever you feel like telling. And don't forget to tell me if Minou still waits for her kitty kibble outside our door. Okay honey, I have to go."

Cathy yelled, "No, no, no. Not yet! Don't go, Daddy! Please don't go!"

The taxi driver opened the door and waited. Joe tossed Cathy up high, caught her, and swung her around his waist, then hugged her for a long time before setting her down. "Now, Cathy, no more tears. That's an order from a master sergeant!" He kissed the top of her head, then lifted up her chin. "And remember, always help your mummy. She's going to miss me too, and you must cheer her up."

Finally he turned to me and held me so hard against him that a button from his coat rammed into my stomach. Our eyes met briefly before he kissed me in the way romantic novels call bruising. The taste of his lips and tobacco remained in my mouth long after the cab disappeared.

Chapter Nineteen

With Joe gone, my life changed. He'd done many tasks almost without my noticing. It began with his giving breakfast to Cathy and taking her to the *maternelle*. Cheerfully, he'd done the marketing, the laundry, and most of the dish-washing. He'd taken care of the bills and managed to keep us on a budget—one that became ever more Spartan toward the end of the month. At this retrenching time, eggs and bread became the mealtime stars: mushroom omelets, eggs and tomatoes, macaroni and cheese, French toast, and something we wistfully called "eggs without bacon." Actually, doing without meat was no big hardship when everything was accompanied by warm, crusty French bread—*grand pains, baguettes*, and our favorite, the ultra-skinny *ficelles*.

Besides taking care of us, Joe had his own political program. A couple of nights a week he attended Communist meetings or union gatherings. Then he studied long hours, day and night, at libraries or at home. Occasionally, bent over criticism of his hero, the godless Denis Diderot, he'd mutter "stupid ass" or "bastard'; if reading Diderot's letters, he might shake his head in delighted disbelief and say "a genius—the man's a century before his time" or simply "God! Oh God!" as though what he'd read was unbearably wonderful. Once in a while, cheerleader style, he'd yell, "You tell 'em Diderot!"

By the end of his year in Paris, he'd completed his thesis on the eighteenth-century French *Encyclopédist* and acquired a master's degree in philosophy. No matter how rushed, he had time to read books, fat quarterlies, and a variety of magazines.

Once I asked his mother, who grew up in the Jewish community of Aleppo, Syria, what Joe had been like as a baby, the fifth of eight children. She looked up at the ceiling while stroking her nose slowly. "Joe"—she pronounced his name "Jaw"—"was good baby. He sleep, he eat, he make, he sleep, he eat. Never give trouble. Not like Al, my last baby, all the time cry, cry, cry. *Ouffe!* Break my ears! One day Ally stop crying. Everybody happy."

She paused and half-smiled. "Joe? He like to make jokes, he smart."

Joe had been the youngest in his law school, having had skipped two grades in grammar school.

"Leedle bit naughty sometime." There was a comfortable silence. She was thinking. "When he was eight, he took big bunch of banana to attic. His sister find him munching, only one banana left, banana peel everywhere. For that, Sam"—his big brother—"call him 'monkey Joe,' so Joe get mad and wrestle him." She made a cluck of acceptance. "Children! Two, three days pass, and they forget to say 'monkey Joe.'" She raised bushy eyebrows and her expression became serious. "Joe very smart," she repeated.

Besides being smart, Joe had a strong sense of duty. Most of us try to be moral and generous; it is, after all, the decent way, the civilized norm for the human condition. Joe viewed all kinds of problems—domestic, labor, national—as an integral part of the life force that needed him, and with an unfailing air of geniality he rose to meet them.

He'd organized our lives in the same spirit, pleased to take responsibility. He'd arranged we meet for dinners with a variety of friends, at one another's digs or at unimpressive bistros that served incredibly cheap meals that weren't bad. He'd provided us with tickets to concerts and, best of all, to plays by Racine, Moliere, and Rostand, all free to us foreign students. But it was he who fetched the tickets from the student center.

Why did we get such a kick out of these plays at a time when we had only the faintest idea what the actors were saying? Possibly we were swept into the seductive aura of the theatre itself, with all its excitement. Even if the French actors sometimes seemed overemotional, their performances were memorable and we were deeply moved by them, often inventing stories to suit the expostulation. Once I wept watching the hero hidden in a filthy sack being beaten mercilessly. I continued to weep despite the rising gales of laughter around me. Joe whispered to me, "It's only a joke, they're just beating on wood." And sure enough, when the man emerged from the sack he looked surprisingly well after such a pounding, and, after shaking himself, launched immediately into a song with lots of jolly *tra-la-la*'s.

Watching the crowd in theatres such as the Comédie-Française was fascinating. The men's faces seemed leaner, more chiseled, more interesting than American faces in subtle ways, suggesting more cerebral activity. I hadn't yet made Paris friends, but in England I'd accepted the notion that French schoolgirls had a mysterious something we sisters across the Channel lacked. While in drizzly gray weather we ran up and down playing fields clutching hockey or lacrosse sticks, or played tennis on soggy grass courts, they stayed indoors. After doing their homework, they crocheted lacy collars, perfected the cooking of omelets, and indulged in witty conversation. Whatever they did resulted in their having something we called "oomph."

Of course, they had a start over us. English as a language is sacred. It has more words than theirs. But French was the language of romance. Some famous man once said "Whenever I hear someone speaking French, I feel I am falling in love." And, in fact, the first time I heard a middle-aged gentleman near me comment in a deep voice "*Oh là-là*," my blood turned warm with excitement.

French women seemed different, more put together, even the older ones. They wore curvy tortoiseshell combs in their upswept hair or a bone barrette at the side of a short coif. A lock of hair might curve onto a smooth cheek in a way that made average cheekbones appear high and high cheekbones even higher. French women wore colorful scarves tied about the neck with nonchalant insouciance.

What struck me was that the majority of them weren't wearing any lipstick at all, or looked as though they weren't, which accentuated the appeal and expressiveness of their eyes, which were skillfully lined and shaded. Perfume was part of their glamour, and when a circle of them talked, the air about them gave off a light fragrance.

During intermissions, while Joe moved about peering at photographs of France's great actors hanging on the walls, I studied the theatregoers. Soon he would join me where I was planted, usually near an animated group who were gesticulating boldly, eyes wide, lips protruding, discussing and interrupting one another with sentences that began with "Yes, yes, but not so fast," or "Why do you think so?"

Once there was a lot of clamor and arguing about what Emily had said. As the civilized battle went on, I tried in vain to identify who Emily might be. Perhaps she wasn't even there. A confident male said, "Emily is mistaken because . . ."—and here he gave a torrent of reasons, almost indecipherable to me, except for the connecting words like "also," "even more," and "the most important thing." Soon he was interrupted and they were all jousting again, voices rising. Finally, a long-haired blonde standing near the wall said quietly, "*Écoute, à mon avis, Émilie a raison, après tout*"—"Listen, in my opinion Emily is right, after all." This harmless remark set off another verbal stampede.

What did those thousands of passionate words amount to? What glittering gems were we missing, Joe and I, outsiders in the heated debate? "Why don't we speak French already?" I whispered to him. Joe lowered his head to one side, brows raised. "You know, sweetie, somehow, but even then—I'm not sure . . ." He left the sentence trailing. I'd never asked him what he meant.

Right now, the theatre seemed as far away as Joe, who was in New York now and—who knew?—might be even at a dance. I pictured him waltzing with a flirtatious woman who resembled Audrey Hepburn. He was steering her toward the side of the room, gliding and circling. Joe was doing "his step"—holding her at arm's length so that they could turn without missing a beat. Her eyes were smiling. How lucky to meet this intelligent giant of a man! Oh, how disloyal he was! How could he, so soon?

That night, after I'd read to Cathy, tucked her in, and learned by heart the meaning and spelling of thirty new French words, I fell like a stone between the heavy linen sheets. I awoke at three, questions swirling in my head. Why did I let him go? Dear old Joe, I miss you already. Life would never be the same. I wanted him back. But did I really? I'd fought hard to have this one-year separation from him, a year which I sensed would split us apart forever.

When I'd married him just shy of eighteen, he, six years older, had made all our decisions. Now I'd changed. It was becoming more and more urgent for me to be self-sufficient, to reach for my potential, to direct my life and Cathy's, even if I made mistakes. Then, too, I liked Joe immensely but didn't love him, not in the way I sensed I could love. He had enriched my life, but he'd hobbled it, too. Right now I was too tired to miss him physically, but I would soon enough.

Lord! My parents and family would soon have to know. Then all hell would break loose. I took a few long, deep breaths, decided to take Cathy to the Eiffel Tower after school tomorrow, and fell back to sleep.

Chapter Twenty

I was scrambling to be on time for the imperatives of the day: Cathy's kindergarten, my early class at the Sorbonne, Cathy's doctor appointments, homework, shopping and cooking, and weekend visits or outings. Each day was so jam-packed that time disappeared, and suddenly it would be time to collect my daughter from the *jardin d'enfants*, her kindergarten on the quai des Célestins. Instead of a garden, it boasted an attractive terracotta courtyard that seemed to heighten the blue of the *tabliers—*smocks—worn by all the children as they ran about playing. Most of the boys wore their hair as long as the girls, kept out of their eyes with barrettes, and one child I'd heard someone call "Pauline," a dazzling beauty with golden ringlets and long-lashed eyes, turned out to be a boy named Paul. He and Cathy became almost inseparable. Cathy told me proudly how the children would try to make Paul blush by shouting *"Oh là-là, Paul! Tu as le béguin pour Cathy."*—"Ah, Paul, you have a crush on Cathy." Paul was a few months older than Cathy.

"And you?" I asked. "Do you like him, too?"

"Yes, I do," she declared. "Not just me. All the girls like him, 'cause of the things he does."

"What is it he does?"

"Well, he can stand on his hands while we count to ten, and Mummy guess what else?"

"What?"

"When he's upside-down, he can lift one hand." She looked up at me, explaining, "Standing on one hand, *maman*—it's hard to do. His face gets so red. None of the other boys can do it. Just Paul."

Cathy's teacher, Mlle Brissard, once told me that whenever there were games, lessons, or dances requiring partners, Paul and Cathy would run to find each other. She'd smiled. "*Les petits! Ils peuvent nous enseigner*"—"The little ones, they can teach us." What had she meant precisely? I never discovered what they could teach us, but she was smiling when she said it.

Around four o'clock, when the parents came for their children, Cathy would be on the lookout for me. As I entered the courtyard she'd yell "*Maman!*" and in seconds a small cannonball would hurl itself at me. Together we would walk up to say *bonsoir* to Mlle Brissard. She had the curious habit of praising to the parent some minor feat the child had performed that day. This time it was "Catherine's rows of *B*'s and *C*'s were excellent, both capitals and small letters. "

When we left the schoolyard the two of us ran and jumped over the cracks in the pavement, played hopping races, first on the left foot, then the right, each checking that the other didn't cheat by alternating the hopping foot. Half the fun for Cathy was to pretend she'd seen me cheating, and so I'd accuse her of cheating. But there would always be a point where, rocking with laughter, she'd have to stop, bent over, holding her stomach.

We'd saunter on, exchanging snippets about our day as we headed toward the busy rue de Rivoli, where the charming *manège*, a merry-go-round of decorated rocking horses and swans, was set into motion to accordion music. Children climbed to the platform excitedly, with an occasional very tiny tot strapped into a swan by a loving parent.

Surprisingly, there were teenagers, too: boys who, after the *manège* began to move, swaggered up to swing their lean legs high over the steeds, cigarettes dangling from their lips.

Cathy always chose the same horse, white with red stripes and a thick mane of chestnut hair, whom she'd named "*Beau Jacques*." She liked to be seated early to have plenty of time with him. She whispered secrets in his ear and braided his hair. She half believed he came to life for her, and I refrained from telling her otherwise.

From her first ride, she'd refused a seat in the beautiful swan's belly, where children her own age usually sat. She'd pulled away, hissing fiercely, "*Le cigne, ce n'est pas amusant!*"—"The swan is not fun!" She was right. In it one simply sat, going around smoothly. No hijinks!

After the attendant checked that her stirrups were not too long and that the strap fit snugly around her waist, she held her head high, her arms around Beau Jacques's neck. But the instant the accordion blared its loud music, she grabbed her pole as it rose and fell.

Like many of the watchers, I hummed or sang along while waving to Cathy, who flicked her hand each time she passed by. Operated and owned by Monsieur Jean, a sturdy middle-aged man who wore a black beret, the carousel was painted in bright colors, with leopards, tigers, and lions showing their teeth from wide, howling mouths that looked more comical than threatening.

The *manège* soon picked up speed, turning faster and faster so that the children shrieked with joy and terror, while the teenagers held their poles with only one hand, their faces bored. Now and then a worried parent would shout, "*Eh bien, Jean, ça suffit! Doucement!*"—"Hey, Jean, that's enough! Go easy!" But Jean knew something about children, and he let it spin fast for a good five minutes.

When the children finally dismounted they were flushed and their eyes shone. Cathy felt she had done something outstanding as she wobbled back triumphantly toward me.

Now was our time to collect things for supper from the local shops, stepping from the *crémerie* to the *boulangerie* to the *boucherie*, where all the shopkeepers knew us.

On the few days I was flat-out tired, we'd pick out treats at the local *charcuterie*, or delicatessen. The dishes in the window made our mouths water. An array of *vol-au-vents*—puff pastry shells filled with chicken, mushrooms, and sweetbreads—were piled on a large blue ceramic plate. A pyramid of giant artichokes sat in a sauce nearby, while the centerpiece was a chunky pie of green onions and bacon decorated with sprigs of parsley.

Inside the small shop, Cathy's eyes flew from dish to dish, mentally tasting each one. At last, with a farewell look toward the *vol-au-vents*, she pointed to the green onion pie and said firmly in

French, "I think I'd like a slice of that one, please." The owner nodded and told her she'd made a good choice, as she'd soon find out. It would be filling. I was hungry and took the same. A man leaning on the counter told me he'd eaten a slice for his lunch and wished me and Cathy "*bon appétit.*"

We had barely taken ten steps when Cathy grabbed my arm and wailed desperately, "Mum, I don't really want the pie."

"Why did you choose it then?"

She looked at the ground, "I don't know. I couldn't decide what else to get."

"Cathy," I said briskly, "you saw Madame slice it. She can't just put it back. Nobody else will want it." I took her hand and began to walk, but she pulled back and stood frowning.

"I don't want it, though." Her voice sounded teary. "I want something else."

"Listen, darling, I don't understand." I crouched to look into her face. "You licked the crumbs off your plate when you ate this same pie last time, remember? We had it with a pear. Your tongue can't have changed its mood so soon."

I thought she'd giggle about her tongue. However, she remained mute.

"Do you know why you don't want it? Perhaps if it's for a good reason I'll see what I can do."

"Well it may not be a good reason."

"Come on, Cath," I said gently. "Out with it." I lifted up my hands in a French way, showing that I was at a loss.

Her voice was high with indignation. "It's all mushy. Ugh." She wrinkled her nose. "Both pieces. While you were talking to the man I saw all the goopy stuff fall into the bag. The pie part isn't under it anymore."

I looked in the paper bag. Absolute mush. "It is a bit squashed," I said matter- of-factly. "The crust has separated from the onions and bacon. But it will still taste good."

She hung her head.

"Look, I don't mind having it for two nights," I said finally. "It is quite expensive, so we can't waste it. How about a vol-au-vent for you tonight?

"Oh Mum, really? Can I?"

"Just this once," I said. "But don't think you'll get away with it again—not even if you see a caterpillar wiggling in it."

"I like caterpillars," she said and put her hand in mine, happy to be returning to the shop.

While I was absorbed and stimulated by most of my classes, I really welcomed my free time: a one-hour lunch hour and a forty-five minute break between the end of classes and picking up Cathy. Moments to wander wherever the spirit took me, such as to the bookstores nearby, where I thumbed through paperbacks by Sartre on existentialism or flipped through gorgeous French art books. Once as I was marveling at the number of paintings by Renoir I'd never known existed, a French student, looking at a Picasso book nearby, muttered "*Superbe!*" Soon we were talking. He said the French reproductions were way ahead of the American ones in rendering a true likeness to the original colors.

In fine weather it took me just minutes to reach the loveliest park in Paris, the Jardin du Luxembourg. As countless students and professors at the Sorbonne had done before me, I basked in this happy park. I saw youngsters sailing their small ships in the boat basin, toddlers digging in the sandpit, and their big sisters rolling wooden hoops down pathways, some showing their younger sisters how a hoop turns with a light tap of a stick.

Or I could feel the sweep of ancient times after a short walk to the Musée de Cluny, standing near the rim of an old stone bath. Often I was the only visitor there, sometimes shivering, with the dust from second-century Roman marble in my nose, surrounded by battered stone blocks on which mosaics of unknown animals were carved.

On the rue Soufflot I could goggle at the neoclassic dome of the Panthéon, a shrine holding the remains of France's most illustrious heroes. Once in a while I had coffee with friends, whom nowadays I saw only on weekends.

One of these was David Ross, a reporter on the English tabloid the *Daily Mail*, which he termed an "ultra-conservative rag." David was one of the few who'd approved of my leaving Joe. "There were parts of you that Joe squelched, without his knowing," he said. Once, after Joe had returned to the United States, David had given me his immaculately clean and ironed handkerchief to wipe my tears before taking me to a cozy bar in a cellar, where we both drank a lot of wine and made deep confessions.

Glynne and Joe, 1950

With Cathy in Paris

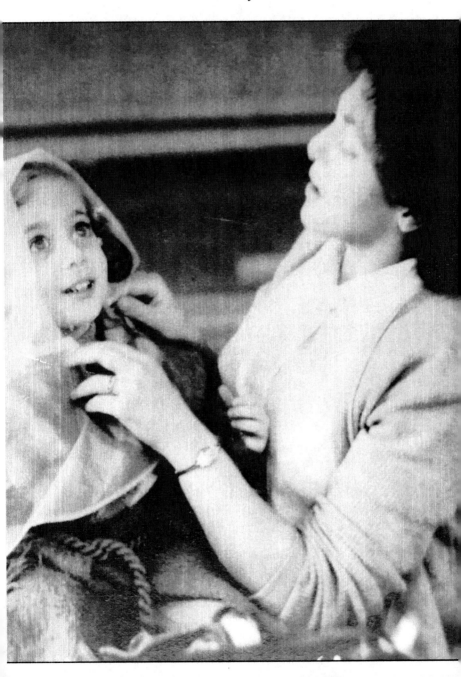

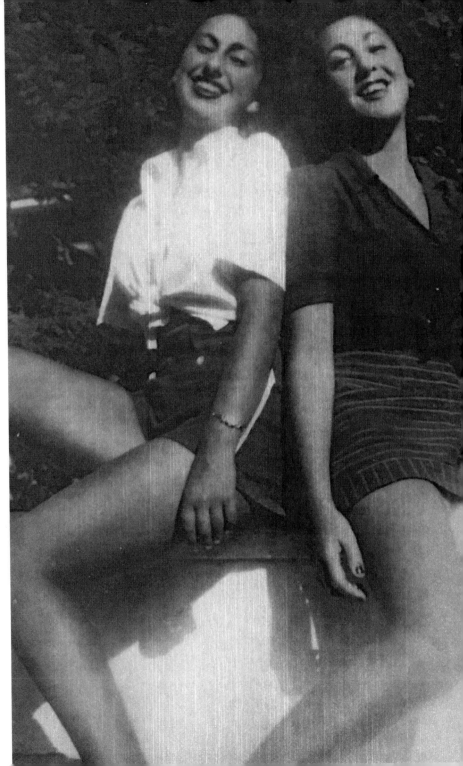

With sister Sally in Greenwich

With Ned in Paris

Maurice

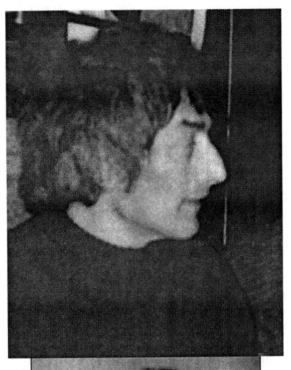

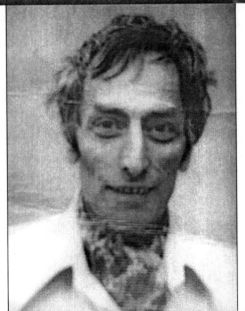

Glynne on the beach

Glynne in necklaces

Chapter Twenty-one

Three weeks after Joe had left, when Cathy and I, carrying our assorted packages, entered the apartment, there was a letter propped up on the narrow table in the hallway. My heart skidded. The handwriting was familiar and dear, as was the "*par avion*" my mother had added to the red-and-blue airmail envelope.

It had arrived—the response to my letter to my parents about my separation from Joe. I had told them I'd be staying on in Paris with Cathy for another year in order to receive my teaching certificate before returning to the States.

I'd tried to soften the blow by saying that when I returned, Joe and I might reconcile our differences and get back together. In presenting this unlikely scenario I felt hypocritical, but it seemed a good way to lessen the initial shock. Had I told my father to his face what I'd done he would have turned apoplectic with rage and begun insulting me in Arabic, while my sweet mother would have patted his shoulder and said something like, "On my life, David, you are going to be ill if you don't stay calm."

After placing her school satchel on a chair, Cathy stood studying the letter with interest. "From my mum, my own mama," I said, pocketing it.

"Does your mama look like you? I've forgotten."

"I've shown you her picture, Cathy, at least a dozen times."

"Yes, but you always say it doesn't look like her. You know," she went on, "I do remember her a bit. When she gave me a big red ball and you and me made up that song. Remember?"

"How could I not?" I gave her my fake severe look, which she'd already learned to turn on me on occasion, and reminded her how we'd sung it in the Jardin du Luxembourg just a few days ago.

"Anyway, Cathy, it's not exactly a song, darling, more like a ditty."
I sang out the first line: "I'd rather have a bouncing ball . . . "

Cathy trilled the next and last line. "Than anything at all!" Then
she grabbed her satchel, announcing that she must do her homework. "It's penmanship, the *J*'s, we must write four of them in
big letters and four in small, and"—shaking her forefinger and
mimicking Mlle Brissard's lofty tones—"*avec un bon écriture*"—
in good handwriting. "Also, in class we've got to recite four names
that start with *J*—Jules, Juliette, Jean, and something else, I forget." She trotted off to the living room.

But she was back in the kitchen as I was beating the eggs
for "scrambles on toast," pattering on about her friend Daphne's sixth-birthday party the next day. It would be Cathy's first
sleepover, and she was excited. "There'll be two boys and three
girls. Paul's coming. He's doing a special trick. Daphne and me
are going to sleep, both in her bed. Not side by side—her feet will
be near my head. So when I wake I'll see her toes." She took a
breath, "I can't wait to pinch them." After a moment, she added,
"And don't forget *not* to pick me from school tomorrow, 'cause
Daphne's mother is coming for us. *Elle va nous chercher*," she
added, to make sure I understood.

"And you, Mlle Cathy, remind me to remind you in the morning
to take your pajamas, unless you want to sleep in your birthday
suit ! And another thing you must take is—"

"Mom," she interrupted, "I know! The present. How about a jig-
saw? I'd love to get one. What do you think?"

I nodded. "Yes, and after she's done with it she can pull it apart
and start again. The more she does it, the better and faster she'll
get. And best of all, we have one already wrapped in my wardrobe.
I bought two on sale, remember? Yours is the squirrel nibbling a
walnut. Hers is a cat eyeing a tortoise."

Later, when she was asleep, I sat on the couch holding the letter, a well-filled packet. It didn't bode well. Not that I was expect-
ing a round of applause from my parents for leaving my husband
and staying on in Paris with my child. But only when I opened
the envelope did I learn the extent of their disapprobation for my
actions, which had taken all my courage, judgment, and honesty

and had so often filled my first year in France with anguish.

My parents, born in Egypt, had settled in Manchester, England, when they were in their early twenties and held tightly to views of a different and earlier culture, both religious and moral. Above all, they considered "Thou shalt love, honor, and obey thy husband for all the days of thy life" as the eleventh commandment. Discussions often took place between them and the five children in Manchester, who on weekends sat with them at the dinner table.

Weekdays the children ate upstairs in the nursery with the nanny. Up until I was ten, we children lived mainly under the watchful eyes of a series of nannies. There was one who assiduously collected old coins, halfpenny bits and farthings, who amused my father. He'd say, "In fifty years, she'll be lucky to exchange that great bag of them for an ice cream cornet."

Pretty Edith, our last nanny, took us to the beach in Wales during our summer holidays, wearing the latest fashion, beach pajamas. I could smell her scent and hear her jaunty way of talking. "It's Jolie Madame." She'd squirt a drop behind my ears. How we children all loved her and her flowered pajamas!

It had been a particular joy to have Edith with us after her predecessor, horrid Mrs. Thornley, who related all our misdeeds to our parents. When we'd faced her with fury and asked, "Why did you tell our father?" she'd look up at the ceiling. "Well now," she'd say, her face becoming owlish, "you'll understand one day. It was for your own good."

To any one of us who, exasperated, flung down his or her pen during homework, proclaiming "This equation is stupid, it can't ever work out," she'd answer, while knitting a hideous brown scarf, "If at first you don't succeed, try, try again."

Still, I'd been quite glad that her earlybirds got the worms. I remember Sally laughing when I'd asked her whether were there any earlybirds in our garden. I thought they were a species, like blackbirds.

I can also see my sister's head turning to one side after I told her my latest Thornley injustice. For instance, I was often the last one at breakfast. "No getting up from the table, young lady, no indeed!

Not until you finish *all* your porridge. There are children in the world who would die for a few spoons of it." Each time I tried to wriggle out of my chair, she'd thrust her hairy arm onto my chest.

Freed eventually and howling miserably, I'd run to Sally. "Nurse Thornley is a pig." Sally would agree, saying something like, "Yes, a rotten fat pig," which made us laugh. But best of all were her next words, which righted all wrongs. "If you're verrry good, Glynne, I'll tell you a fairy tale and give you a lemon drop."

In no time I'd be a happy goblin of four again as I sucked away blissfully, inhabiting Sally's fairyland. There wasn't much to worry about in her plots. By the end of the tale, she would always find a way for poor Twinkletoes or Tinkerbell to be invited to the acorn feast after all. And everyone always lived happily ever after.

When we ate downstairs with our parents, Pa would ask us questions about our schools, our teachers, and our sports. At times, our answers made him reel with laughter, but we rarely understood why. Eddy, seven years older than I, would always bring up risky topics. Once he asked, "Pa, I've been thinking a lot about this. What actually do you think is the meaning of life?"

At first our father was genial, more or less. "Well, boy, that's a strange question. You breathe, you see wondrous sights—the sky, the sea—you laugh and play, you work hard at school, and you obey your father and mother. That's the best meaning."

I waited, holding my breath. "What I'm asking," Eddy said, "is why actually are we put on this earth?"

Pa turned to my mother near him and shook his head. "What can you say to a boy who has no sense?" His voice was stern as his eyes swiveled round to rest on Eddy. "You *ja-hass* [moron]. God didn't supply us with the meaning. He gave us the whole thing itself. Be grateful he included you and that all of us were given the gift of life. It's up to each of you to follow the right pathway, one guided by your parents. Now do you understand?"

Oh, please, Eddy, stop, I'd pray inwardly, knowing he wouldn't. "So okay, Pa, would you say that most people are satisfied?"

Pa shrugged at my mother again, who placed one of her small hands near his lapel. "How can you answer such a silly question, Freda?" To Eddy, he thundered, "That's enough, boy! No more of this rubbishy talk. Do you hear?" His voice cut through the air. Solemnly he addressed us. "The Almighty created this world and the people in it. At times"—he paused and continued almost dreamily—"perhaps he tests us to find out which ones are good and which are evil. It's like an exam. Some pass, others fail."

Many discussions were truncated by my father's quick temper. And my mother was often torn, trying to placate both him and us. Often I wanted to say something, but my family always interrupted, and she occasionally would smile at me, saying, "Everyone hush. Give the little one a chance." So I held the stage and made the most of it. Usually I stopped because someone made a funny face at me, which started me laughing. During one of my rare utterances, I announced, "I don't want our gardener to keep killing rabbits. They have feelings like us." I was about seven and so overcome by my speech I began to cry. My mother half-smiled at me before saying to my father, "Now, what do you think of that, David?"

Another time, Pa talked about honoring one's parents. "God's commandment was 'Love thy father and thy mother!'" he said piously.

"But Pa," Eddy commented, "you can't command everlasting love, surely." Since this was a purely theoretical discussion, my father, the patriarch, could afford to be easygoing, and after clearing his throat said, "Well, boy, remember, there are many kinds of love, of which marital love is the truest. The wife becomes a part of the husband, the husband a part of the wife. Like your mother and me."

"But," Eddy persisted, "you and Ma sometimes quarrel. At that moment do you truly love each other?"

"What a *ja-hass* you are," he roared, forgetting he'd once confided his wish to us to be as calm as an Englishman. "What do they teach you at school? A disagreement has nothing to do with love." Again his voice was gentle. "A wife and a husband suffer together and rejoice together, so that in time their love is deeper and is full of remembering. And so it becomes a more binding love. You understand, children?"

At the time I was deeply touched by his words. I'm not sure

about my siblings, though they put on thoughtful countenances.

Occasionally Eddy would try to be tactful. "Okay, you may be right, but Pa, allow the wind of doubt to enter your mind." Pa frowned ominously, waiting for the tirade of words that would challenge him. "I mean," Eddy said, "isn't it possible that too much suffering might destroy love instead of increasing it?"

To which my less-than-tolerant father would seek support from his wife. Breathing hard, he asked, "Can you tell me, Freda, where does this boy get all his rubbish from?" My mother fluttered her eyes and gently shrugged, while we children, pink from holding in our laughter, would get busy with our knives and forks.

In the nursery, there were no holds barred. We laughed at off-color jokes, related stories that we thought screamingly funny or terrible, and all acted out the hero's role in the last film seen at the local cinema, accompanied by a woman at the piano who played at breakneck speed at frightening moments in the film. And upstairs we could always grumble at the absurd curfews set by our parents and at their latest decisions.

Yet I loved my father, in a conflicted kind of way. His deep-seated customs and rooted Arabic-Jewish beliefs were often archaic and daunting. Yet he was just: scrupulously fair in his treatment of us and in his presents, pocket money, and rewards. Each week he'd ask Mummy, the nanny, and the maids which child had behaved the best, who had been kind, and so on. There were three prizes. First was a silver sixpence, second was a silver threepenny bit, and third was a penny. I was five when it began, and I didn't know exactly what you had to do to merit a prize, other than eating everything on your plate.

I almost never got the sixpence. Even after manfully eating the slimy barley in an otherwise wonderful vegetable soup and shelling large numbers of peas, I only made the silver threepenny bit. Yet I was so overjoyed that I tossed it up in the air and caught it again and again all evening.

Eating everything on one's plate carried enormous weight and was equated with good behavior. So likely as not, the greediest of us got the sixpence. Either the nanny or the maid would threaten, "You must eat your plate clean before leaving the table." When I was kept there I used to scream loudly, hoping my parents in the dining room would hear me and come to the rescue. Then nanny would hush me and let me get down and play. My parents, absent from most meals with us, would not have approved of this plate-cleaning ritual. Yet we rarely told tales about the nannies, even when they hit us. We were too proud.

My mum was different from my father. She was pliable and could be swayed. Yet she, too, was taught from the time she could read the laws written by men to subjugate women. She, like my father, was an Arabic Jew, and the most important thing in her life from the time she could walk was that she would become a good wife who took care of her children, respected her husband, and submitted to his decisions. Although I rarely confided deep thoughts to her, I loved her. I loved her laughter, her touch, her way of talking, her gestures. And how she liked to cook! There's a picture in my mind of her and her friends in the kitchen, all the women stuffing things with meat and rice and telling rude stories in Arabic that convulsed them with laughter. What a good story-teller she was, too—in her own style of English as well as in Arabic. Sometimes she treated us to tales of her early days in Cairo with her seven younger siblings and her strict parents, to our furious indignation. She would end by saying, "And you think your father is strict? After my father, he is a piece of velvet."

It was time to open my mother's letter. As always, it was mostly my father's thoughts: he had weak eyes and relayed to my mother what he wanted to say.

"My dear Glynne," it began. "Thank you for your letter of the 8th. I'm afraid your father is not very pleased with the way you are acting." There followed a list of criticisms of my unbecoming behavior. I half-read them, rolling my eyes, then turned to the final two paragraphs, which he'd directly dictated.

"Now this is what you are to do, child. You must book either a ship or a plane to bring you and your daughter back here immediately. I will be glad to wire you whatever money you need for expenses. If you are not back here by the end of three weeks, I will disown you. I will cast you out. You will no longer be my daughter, which means I will be disowning you and you will no longer have a father. Furthermore, you're Joe's wife and so you must remain with him at all costs. A woman breaking up her family is unforgivable. There are two exceptions for a separation. One, the man is an irredeemable alcoholic. The other is he is threatening to take your life."

My mother wrote a gentle postscript, saying that she would be leaving for Paris in about two weeks, as she was taking my brother Max to Cairo to look for a bride "because Max is nearly thirty and always goes with loud, rude girls. The young women he will meet in Egypt will be intelligent and modest, and all will want to be a good wife and bear him many children. (Better than being an old maid taking care of a father, isn't it?) I will stay with Sophie"—Sophie was my mother's sister—"in Paris for one night, while Max will fly to my brother's house in Cairo, where I will meet him. And so, darling, I will visit you from Sophie's house and see you are all right. Please listen to your father. You know, he usually knows best."

There followed her usual ending to all of her letters, which none of us had the heart to correct: "Best wishes, dolly, from your lovely mother." It still could evoke a quick smile.

A flood of self-pity threatened to wash over me. All of the conflict and anxiety, the fighting with Joe for what was important to me for so long, would be starting up again, this time in a battle with my parents.

I needed a strong cup of tea. Waiting for the water to boil, my eyes glazed with fatigue, the doorbell rang. Was Mme Doucet back from her daughter's house already? She wasn't due back for three days. But it couldn't be: she had a key.

God, I hoped it wasn't Théo, Joe's weird friend. He'd started giving Mme Doucet injections in her large thighs to help her walk. I wriggled my feet into my wool slippers and, assuming an air of total exhaustion, pulled the door open halfway. Then I heard my mother's voice: "Glynne! Glynne dolly, where are you?"

I opened the door wide and flung my arms around her. "Mum! Oh Mum!"

The *minuterie* light had switched itself off, and although she had found the door and the bell, she had turned around in the dark and was facing a corner. Her tremulous reply made me cry and laugh too. Her dark eyes were swimming as I held her hand and pulled her inside. She pushed a big brown paper parcel at me ("For little Caty"). In her tweed suit she was as petite and slim as ever, and her cheeks were pink. She never wore makeup, but when she was excited her eyes became luminous and bright.

I pushed her gently into the armchair, and she kept her small hand in mine. She was half-laughing, half-crying as her eyes searched my face. "Oh Glynne, Glynne darly! Why are you such a naughty girl?"

I sat on a low stool facing her. "Oh, Mum," I said. "I'm not. Not really, you know, I..." But I couldn't talk. My head fell forward and I started crying.

She said gently, "Don't cry, silly-billy. Nothing to cry for." She rose to kiss me on my forehead several times. I ended my last snivels and gave her a watery smile. "There," she said, "dat's better." My mother never could pronounce the *th* sound. "And Caty? How is she? Is she well? I don't suppose I'll get to see her before I leave." She glanced at her watch. "We have an hour together, a bit more maybe; mustn't miss the plane! The taxi is coming here at eleven. It takes me to your Auntie Sophie's house. Poor darling, she's getting up early to go with me to the airport at six o'clock in the morning." She looked at me entreatingly and once again asked the question to which she really didn't expect a reply. "But Glynne, darling, tell me, why are you such a naughty girl? Why don't you listen to your father? He wants what's best for you."

Before I could respond she put her hand to her breast and said, "I'm dying for a cup of tea. Dat cup Sophie gave me, a French kind, *ouffe*, tasted like Soir de Paris perfume. Its scent is still in my troat."

We sat in the kitchen because time was short. My blue teapot lay in the middle of the table alongside a jug of milk, a sugar bowl and two cups and saucers. As I poured, my mother dug into her immense bag and handed me a tin of Arabic pastries, including baklava and grabies. These taste heavenly and need time and skill to make. I tucked in ravenously. I knew she'd never eat more than one. (Once I'd told Joe that she ate like a bird, and he'd said, "Do you know that birds often eat twice their weight daily?")

She lifted the blue-rimmed cup to her mouth and took a sip. "Mmmm. Very nice."

"It's called 'Royal Family' tea and actually comes from London. And it is good enough for a queen."

"Now darly," she went on, "it's time for you to tell me what am I to tell your father." She popped a small piece of pastry into her mouth and waited.

I cleared my throat. "Mum, please try to break it to him gently. I'm not coming back right away. I need this certificate from the Sorbonne in order to find a job. I'll be home in a year's time."

My mother was shocked. Her face seemed to shrink with disappoint- ment. "But your father will disown you. You won't be his child anymore."

"Yes I will. I'll always be his child. He planted the seed."

"But sweetheart, he won't"—she scratched her head, searching for the right word—"*acknowledge* you as his daughter. You won't be part of our family anymore."

"Mum, do you in your wildest imagination see Eddy or Max, Lulu or Sally avoiding me?"

She lifted her hands. "I didn't say dat."

"And won't you always be my mother?"

Unexpectedly, she began to laugh "Well, I suppose so. You are my baby, the youngest. But... " her voice trailed off. "Your father will not be pleased."

"I'll write to him," I promised. "I'll try hard to explain matters in the best way I know how. And now I'm going to wake Cathy. You cannot go without seeing her."

Her face lit up. "Leave her to sleep," she said politely.

"Indeed! She's dying to see you."

Soon Cathy, wearing the new woolen dressing gown that was in the parcel, was dancing about the room. "It's so light I can fly in it!" she shouted, pink from sleep.

My mother watched her jumping and hopping and said, "That child, so light-haired. And where did she get her blue eyes? Tell me where she came from. Heaven?"

"She came from right here," I said, patting my tummy.

Cathy, now in her grandma's lap, kissed her and thanked her

for the present. "How did you know blue was my favorite color?"

My mother answered her in French. "I bought it to match your eyes. Nothing but the best for my granddaughter, *ma petit-fille.*"

Cathy was puzzled. "But isn't your *petite fille* Mummy?"

"Your mama is *ma fille.* You are *ma jolie petite-fille. Tu comprends?*"

Cathy nodded. *"Ah oui."*

Then my mother whispered in my ear. "And the best thing for every child is to have a mummy and a daddy. So please, darly, please—try to make up with Joe."

Chapter Twenty-two

The next morning I was awakened by a pungent smell. Madame usually made her coffee after we were gone, so I knew we'd overslept. Flinging my dressing gown over my shoulders, I hurried over to Cathy's curtained alcove. She was snoring faintly. I stroked her head. Startled, she sprang up to a sitting position, rubbing her eyes.

"Oh Mum!" She scratched her head. "I was just climbing up my big birthday cake. You and grandma were watching me. And I'd almost got to the top and was just going to cut it. And . . . "

"And?"

"You came and busted the dream."

"Darling! Awfully sorry, but we're terribly late."

"Yes, but I never got to eat even a crumb of my own cake!"

I kissed the nape of her neck.

"*Dis donc!*" She liked this snappier French for "listen" or "I say" but went on in English, swinging her legs to the floor while yawning. "I'm so sleepy. All I want is to go back in my birthday-cake dream."

"Well, you can't. Remember, it's only a dream cake. And I'm just as sleepy as you are. But sweetheart, do you want Mlle Brissard to lock you out of school again? Today, on your first sleepover date?"

She cheered up at the word "sleepover," and a few minutes later we were both dipping hunks of baguette into our warm *cafés au lait*, our cheeks bulging as we bolted them down. Then off we went, clattering down our four flight of stairs. To the exercise book in her satchel Cathy had added her flannel pajamas, her toothbrush, her comb, and the gift she'd wrapped in brown paper for Daphne, on which she'd crayoned six purple balloons.

Out on the street she nibbled at the small "butty"—bread and butter—I'd put in her hand just before we left. She loved saying "butty," a word possibly coined by Welsh miners, who gave these crusts to their children to stave off hunger before supper. In Lancashire, where I was born, some of our nannies would give us butties as a treat when supper wasn't quite ready.

Soon Cathy and I were racing each other, while managing to leap over the cracks in the pavement as well, so that we actually reached her kindergarten nearly on time. But seeing no children in the playground, I said, "Now run like the wind!" and gave her a quick hug.

She galloped up the school pathway and in one jump landed on the step leading to the front door. She turned to me, her face filled with glee, and waved wildly before entering.

Now it was my turn to make tracks so as not to be late for my class at the Sorbonne. My thoughts were swirling about my wonderful mum. I thought of her fright at being alone in the dark, and how swiftly her fear had changed to gaiety when she'd seen me.

I relived the previous night's empathy between us, remembering how easily we'd talked, sipping our tea, facing each other. Actually, we'd never done anything like this before. Had being away from my father liberated her?

As I hurried along, a pale sun was pushing through the gray clouds. I could almost hear her voice saying, "You are my baby, the youngest."

Then I pictured my parents at the long dining table, my father at the head. He'd just made one of his apoplectic pronouncements: "If that girl doesn't leave Paris within three weeks, she can go to hell for all I care!"

A pause, and then my mother's answer: "David, for my sake, please don't excite yourself. I saw with my own eyes what she's doing in Paris. She's a good girl. Busy all day in school. Her room is like a library, books and papers wherever you look. On my life, David, she's not at all interested in men. She's the whole time cooking and studying and taking care of her little girl."

Not exactly true, but my mum could be the soul of tact when

facing my father. I imagined her finally saying, "Once she gets her certificate she'll come straight home. David, *abousa*—I kiss her. "For my sake, don't be so hard." She might even press her small hand against his arm. I didn't dare imagine his response.

I'd reached the Sorbonne and was already climbing up the old stone steps. As I entered my classroom, the bell chimed. Returning Ned's jaunty smile, I exchanged *bonjours* with several of my classmates. Sliding into my desk, I saw a scrap of white paper sticking out of my empty inkwell. It read: "Say, how about lunch? It's a bona fide invitation! Ned."

I caught his eye and mouthed "I can't." I already had an appointment. Dammit! I'd have liked to have lunch with him. So I did something rather brash. I wrote him a note: "Please wait for me after class."

Mme Cerise, who taught us "La Poésie Française," had arrived, her high heels clickety-clopping down the wooden aisle up to the teacher's desk. In English, her name would be Mrs. Cherry. She was tall, with a generous mouth in a birdlike face. Her dark hair was always elegantly cut, so whenever she tossed her head, which she frequently did, it fanned out in the air. Although I tossed my head before the mirror just as she did, my hair never seemed to fan out like hers.

Her enjoyment of French Romantic poetry was indisputable, but the words were unfathomable. We listened politely to her voice as it rose and fell, and sometimes even shook with emotion. We watched her brows rise, her eyes widen. We watched as she swayed from side to side, at times closing her eyes as though caught up in utter bliss, while we tried to figure out how to look when we understood nothing.

Until now, her poems had harked back to another age. Today, she recited a more recent, and seemingly easier, poem, by Edmond Rostand, the author of *Cyrano de Berrgerac*, that was written in 1911. It had a simple title, "Le Petit Chat"—"The Little Cat."

When she asked at the end, as she always did, if we had enjoyed it, we examined the ceiling before making our "yes" or "no" wrist gestures. Ned answered with a French idiom: "*De temps en temps*"—"Sometimes."

Disappointed, she attempted to convey the poem's depths, plowing into terrible English. "It ees, *eh bien*, 'ee want 'er to know when she 'ees old, 'ow much 'e love 'er when she was young. So is a leetle sad." We tried not to smile, but soon we were giggling. It was a release. Rostand had kept us silent for a long time.

Mme Cerise exclaimed, "I think you have understood nothing. Nothing at all." Oddly, her lament was one of the few things we did understand.

Now Madame held a black-covered paperback book, while enunciating slowly in French, "These are the words of Jacques Prévert. The book is entitled '*Paroles*.' Prévert is known for being avant-garde and brilliant. He's written dialogue for many films, some of which perhaps you've seen: *Les Enfants du paradis,* perhaps? *Quai des brumes*?" These were films we all knew. We leaned in.

"And here is one of his proverbs," she continued, reading in English. "'An orange on the table, your dress on the rug, and you in my bed, sweet present of the present, cool of night, warmth of my life.'" Somebody clapped. We understood this poet.

She continued, "Has anyone heard of *"Les Feuilles mortes"*? Several hands shot up. Most of us knew the song "Autumn Leaves" but hadn't known the lyrics were by Prévert. Quite unselfconsciously, Madame started humming the tune. Liona, the tall blond from Sweden, knew the lyrics and sang in a sweet, fluty voice. Others joined in. I wished I knew the words.

Later I'd buy the 45 RPM and play it on Cathy's phonograph.

After class, Ned was waiting for me in the hallway.

"I'm terribly sorry I can't meet you for lunch," I said. "I already have an appointment." I paused, took a breath, and added brazenly, "But I'm actually free this evening."

There was a silence. Had I been untoward? Then he grinned, some of his blond hair flopping over his forehead.

On the way home I wondered what I'd wear that evening. I was glad I'd been forward.

Chapter Twenty-three

Epicurus said that a true friend is someone who allows you to be essentially who you are. With David, the English reporter, I couldn't be anybody else. When we were together we spoke easily about whatever came to mind, with many interruptions and few pauses.

He'd always jump up and greet me with some wild compliment. Today, although he'd seen my gray-and-white wool dress half a dozen times, his dark brown eyes looked approving. "That crimson belt on your waist, it's so right. Well, but of course you know you're a smasher."

I knew nothing of the kind. I was attractive, slim, with big, lively eyes. A smasher was my English friend, Audrey: tall, with glossy red hair, a wide smile, and slanted green eyes that spelled fun and mischief. The one who just a few months earlier, when we lived in Passy, had dragged me to an abyss of hatred and jealousy. Amazing that we'd parted good friends. I often pictured her at the lectern at Oxford, delivering a brilliant lecture on Keynes's theory on aggregate demand to first-year university students. She would be coolly aware that the focus of the young men hovered on the unbuttoned neckline of her scholar's gown. I couldn't help smiling.

"Why are you grinning?" David's voice brought me back.

Okay. If he thought I was a smasher, who was I to argue? "Allow me to purr over your compliment," I said.

Soon we were munching *croques monsieurs* and *cafés crèmes* at Le Voltaire. I told him I was going to meet a chap called Ned for dinner that night, my first date since Joe had left.

"Congratulations! Now, don't go falling in love with him—or anyone. Give yourself time, breathe in the oxygen, dance, see more of Paris. Remember, this is your time to be single."

"*D'accord*," I agreed. "Anyway, I doubt if Ned even knows how to dance."

"Is he a Limey?"

"No, a Yank."

"Another one?" David pulled a face and imitated a Cambridge accent. "My deah! What's wrong with a decent English chap? Oh well, can't be helped. Better luck next time."

He bent forward. "Now Glynne, I've got a tidbit of news for you, too. Tamara and I . . . Well, we're about to become respectable."

"You wouldn't know how!" I scoffed. Tamara was my babysitter. He had met her at my apartment, and they'd been magnetized by each other. In less than four months, they'd made their vows in the town hall. I'd been one of the four witnesses. "Well...don't stop." I said, as David seemed to be daydreaming. "How will you be respectable?"

"Can you believe that we're joining the mums and dads club?" He gave an abashed grin, adding in a low voice, "Just between us, Glynne—we're not advertising it, yet. Tamara is only in her third month."

I leaped up. "David! Some tidbit. That's such amazingly marvelous news." I stretched over the table and planted a kiss on his mouth.

I saw that he was flushed. I hadn't meant it to be a sensual kiss, but somehow it had ended up that way, and I'd been the instigator, holding my mouth on his warm lips. Why do I do these things? I felt ashamed because I could tell he felt guilty, in spite of his joshing comment: "You must promise to do that for every baby Tamara and I have!"

"I'll do it twice if it's twins," I responded. "But David, what an incredibly young father you'll be. People will think the baby is your brother or sister. And Tania, is she feeling okay?"

"She's actually blooming, and she gets better looking every day. I catch her dreaming contentedly in the armchair sometimes. Women, you know, once they've made a cozy nest, they want to fill it. Didn't you do the same?"

Actually, I didn't. Cathy had swum her way in through double contraceptives. But I wasn't about to embark on that story.

"Tamara misses you and sends you, as always, gigantic hugs for having introduced us," David said.

We sat thinking our own thoughts until he broke the silence. "Now see what your meddling has wrought!" He laughed.

I didn't need to ask him if he was happy. It was spilling out of him.

"You've been a bad girl lately, Glynne. You haven't visited us. We miss Cathy, too, so make time for us. Come whenever you want. Weekends are best; one of us is usually home."

I said I would love to, adding, "It won't be that long before you'll be wanting me and Cathy as your babysitters."

Glancing at his watch, he leaped up. "God, tempus does fugit , and I'm due at a meeting near the Opéra."

On the street we hugged. I wasn't about to kiss him on the mouth again. "Well done, David," I said, squeezing his shoulder. "Can I please be the godmother?"

"I've never known quite what a godmother's duties include. To spoil them, I suppose. Of course you can." He waved, turned quickly, and started running.

I decided to go home before meeting Ned. Cathy and I had no clean underwear, for one thing; I'd have time for a bath, too, in that preposterous galvanized tub. I might even do a mote of homework, write a letter, or take a quick nap before meeting him.

I brushed my dress and spent far too long hunting for my eyelash curler, which I found in one of my slippers after a frantic ten minutes. It was too late now for much folderol, so I settled for a few strokes of mascara, powdering my nose, and applying two coats of my darker lipstick. My cheeks were naturally rosy. I grabbed my black-and-white-checked coat. Once I'd loved it so. Now I couldn't see why.

Ned and I almost collided under the portico of La Bonne Bouffe. "Glynne! *Bonsoir.*" His eyes looked even bluer under the lamp. "I was wondering which tree to hide behind until you arrived. Figured you'd think me gauche if I came early."

I was pleased to see him. "Here we are, amazingly, both on time." I added, "I really wouldn't have thought you gauche. Quick, we'd better join the queue."

He grabbed my arm and we got behind a man with a ragged gray beard who kept pointing to the sky as he talked to his friend. She would attempt to interrupt with a vivacious "*Mai, Bertrand, voyons,*" every so often, but he never once stopped to hear her out.

Ned bobbed his head in the man's direction, whispering, "Not until he's eating will she get her chance to talk." Then, looking at me, "My! You are elegant! I've never seen you dressed up." He grinned. "Not that you don't look elegant all the time."

"The same to you!" He was wearing a long tan trench coat that made him look even taller than his six feet. Later on, I'd see the wooly argyle vest that some woman must have knitted for him. Just when we were comfortably talking, still outside, the restaurant door opened, and the rosy-faced owner beckoned us in. Once inside, we could hear her bellowing to the those outside, "You've come to a restaurant, not a race track. Patience." She came back in.

A dark man in an apron appeared. "*Bonsoirs, messieurs dames, Vous préférez en bas ou en haut*?" he asked. Would you prefer to stay here or go upstairs? "How about the *en haut, s'il vous plait.*" Ned addressed us both, me and the waiter, who said, "Please," pointing to the staircase. At the top, a woman with immense earrings and smile to match ushered us to a table in the center.

"Madame, would it be possible to have a corner table, do you think?" Ned spoke with a certain assurance in English.

I thought Madame was about to say "*Je suis désolée mais—*" the equivalent of "sorry'" —but noticing a couple standing up ready to leave, she changed it to, "*Mais oui, Monsieur, pourquoi pas?*"

She seated us at a table, hurrying back to lay a clean cloth and silverware. The paintings on the walls up here were even more arresting than downstairs. Framed opposite me, a woman's pink foot was standing on a man's face. And near to it was a giant seagull waving frenzied wings above a group of nudes matter-of-factly eating slices of something red—meat or melon?

Both of us now were seated, awaiting menus, eyeing the paintings around us. "Hey, Glynne! There's a naked fellow behind you," Ned announced, lighting up a Gauloise. I turned. Behind my back hung a canvas of a handsome young lad holding a glass of wine. His only clothing was a blue kerchief around his neck.

"An ideal style for summer," Ned murmured.

Between the paintings covering the walls, a faded terracotta color was visible, and the floor's polished wooden planks must have come from another century. I loved the atmosphere here, and Ned, too, was taking it all in. I took the chance to pass on to him what I'd been told, that the owner gave struggling artists three or four meals in exchange for a painting—on condition it was at least a foot square. He laughed, "Maybe those who paint nudes get an extra meal. There are so many."

We listened to the hub of student voices rising in the smoky air, mingling with their laughter. At the tables everybody seemed occupied in a multiplicity of tasks: animatedly talking, listening, heads shaking in disagreement or nodding approval, and always much gesticulating with forks and knives. Morsels of bread were flung onto plates, retrieved by fingers that mopped up the last traces of sauce then eaten with vigor. This dipping caper would not have been countenanced across the channel, but by now I'd learned to mop up equally efficiently, and with the same pleasure.

Our waitress pointed to the blackboard propped against the wall. "There you have *les spécialitiés du jou, le prix fixe.*" She dragged a stained menu from her pocket. "Otherwise, you can choose from this, the normal one." She flashed us a smile, saying she'd soon return.,

Peering over to look at the blackboard, Ned said, "Anthony and Meg, the friends I live with, went gaga about the specials here. Their one complaint was waiting."

"I think it sharpens one's taste buds," I said. "When I have friends for dinner, somehow it's nowhere near ready. So when my rather ordinary stew finally gets served, it receives rhapsodic cries and moans of joy."

He didn't answer because just then a waitress passed by holding two plates of shrimp on high, leaving a trail of heavenly scent in the air. My tummy was getting excited. Ned was following the scent, his head turning about a hundred degrees as he sniffed the garlicky shellfish, ""*Zut!* Get a load of that!" he said. "Are you hungry?"

"Ravenous," I said, eyeing the blackboard hopefully for *crevettes*, or shrimp. They weren't there. In fact, the prix fixe, written in chalk, was limited to either of two complete meals.

For roughly six and a half dollars one could have either *paté de campagne* or Greek mushrooms to start, followed by *coquilles St. Jacques* (scallops) or *pot-au-feu* (beef stew) with *tarte aux pommes* (apple tart) for afters. A *pichet,* or flask of wine, holding three glasses cost one buck for ordinary wine and two for a better vintage.

Mlle placed a clean checked cloth and clay pot of anemones, red and deep mauve, with black centers, on our table.

"My favorite flowers —brought to us." I beamed in delight.

Ned studied them, dipping his head over the vase. "Though they don't smell much, they are exquisite" He paused and said, "I'm getting pot in the fire, whatever it is, as a main dish."

"It's beef boiled with carrots and garlic in the pot, you can throw anything you want into it, too, like old parsley or wilted celery, a soft tomato, even a leathery bit of cabbage."

Ned grimaced,. "It sounds quite a treat. I can't wait to try it with leathery cabbage and dead parsley some day in your house!".

During the meal we kept up a lively patter. "Are you a sportsman—football, tennis, basketball?" I asked.

"Well, I play pool."

I looked back at him, baffled.

"You've heard of snooker or billiards? Those games you play with wooden sticks called cues on an oblong green baize table?"

"Oh," I said, "I think I've heard of it."

"How about sometime I tell you the fine points of pool in exchange for a rundown on that unfathomable game cricket?"

"Perhaps. Is it fun playing pool?"

"Yep," said Ned laconically. "Also lucrative. I play for money."

"Are you a gambler?"

"One might say so. I play bridge for stakes, too. And pretty high! And I play Ping-Pong too."

"But Ned, surely you don't play innocent Ping-Pong for money, do you?"

"Not all the time," he said, quickly. "If you like, we can have a game at the American Center sometime. Not for money," he added hastily.

Once outside the restaurant we stood facing each other. I was ferreting in my coat pockets for my gloves when my wrists were swiftly seized—and then swiftly released.

"Were you digging for your gloves?" he asked, almost accusingly.

I nodded. "It's not that cold. I do it mostly from habit. Wear gloves, I mean."

"Well, what would you say to cutting your habit in half, just for now? Wear one—say, the right glove. How about that?" He smiled.

I twigged. This fellow wanted to hold hands with me. Shall I let him? Do I want to? Even as I pondered, my fingers went ahead of me, wriggling out of my left glove and leaving it bare for the taking. And why not? Handholding isn't an act of wild passion. Besides, I realized I wanted to touch his hand.

And with Ned's warm palm against my cold one, we began heading toward the Jardin du Luxemburg. I'd never been there at night. Gently, he pushed his fingers through mine so that our fingers were enlaced. We walked along, me slightly tipsy from my glass of Vouvray, both comfortably in step, not saying much.

We'd almost reached the park's wrought-iron gates when he suddenly stopped.

"Wait," he said, almost brusquely, removing his hand.

"What? Why?"

"I need to ask you something." He sounded serious. What now? I stiffened. I hoped he wasn't about to get all melodramatic about nothing.

"Okay, what?"

"Glynne, tell me, did you like the feeling of my hand in yours?"

My heart sank. What was driving this fellow? Where was the easygoing Midwesterner I'd taken him for? I lobbed his question back. "And you? How did mine feel in yours?"

"I asked first."

I bit my lip, trying not to smile. I thought of how nicely his hand had fit in mine. And he'd not grasped it as though for dear life, nor held it limply. Best of all, as well as providing warmth, it had sent a low current of excitement through me.

"Out with it, Glynne. Are you daydreaming? Or conjuring something to say that will spare my feelings?"

"I was miffed when you suddenly stopped dead right before the park with no warning, like a sort of dictator." I was breathing deeply. "It so happens that your hand was giving me warmth and assurance, but don't let that go to your—"

"No, it won't go to my head, heaven forfend!" He reclaimed my hand. "I've given warmth and assurance to a gal who's already self-assured, just by holding her hand. Now that's not so bad." He paused. "And don't think me addled for stopping like that." He lowered his head. "Think, Glynne, how could we get started on a decent relationship if you hadn't liked holding my hand?"

Better not mention that this entire year I'd been battling to be free of a "decent relationship."

"Tell me," I said, "have you ever *not* felt good when you're holding a woman's hand?"

He shot back, "Yes, actually I have. Yet I still pursued her—the woman—and it soon turned to ashes. And thus my 'hand edict' came into being."

I looked into his eyes. "Anyway, you still haven't said. How did you feel holding my rough southpaw?"

Instead of answering, he fluttered his free hand theatrically on his raincoat over his heart and closed his eyes.

I laughed. He called me a cold cynic.

When we arrived at the gates of the park we looked at each other in disbelief and began laughing. They were locked. The park had been closed for hours. Neither of us had even considered that possibility.

We headed for the Gibert Jeune bookstore on the Place Saint-Michel, close to the metro station. Soon I became immersed in the beginning of a Henri Troyat novel.

Ned interrupted me excitedly. "Look what I've found." He was carrying a large book in his hands. "We'll see the Jardin du Luxembourg tonight after all."

And we did, side by side bent over a table, studying the photographs of the park and reading bits of its history. We felt knowledgeable recognizing so many things: the boat basin, the puppet theatre, the statues, the Palais du Luxembourg, and the Manège Garnier, built by the same architect who designed the Opéra.

"Listen to this, Ned," I said, reading a caption: "'These gardens were open only to royalty before the revolution.' I expect they wouldn't have let the likes of us in."

"Who'd want to mix with a bunch of inbred dullards, anyway?" he said loftily.

"But Ned, think of those twelve-course dinners and graceful dances. And how about the gorgeous dresses? And the men dressed in purple and pink silk."

Ned's eyes wandered over my face. "I knew you were a hedonist. It's one of your attractions."

We left the bookstore. We'd scarcely taken a few steps when a nearly full moon burst from behind the clouds. It glinted over the boulevard, the balconies, and the steeples and turned the bark of the chestnut trees, with their many ribbed boughs, into streaks of silver. We looked up, excited by the extraordinary light. Ned squeezed my hand. "You know, it's comforting to find things like the moon always up there, in its right place."

I was pleased by the observation and smiled.

We'd reached the metro station. "Like to take a promenade?" he asked.

"No," I said firmly. "It's been a lovely evening, Ned, but I'm avalanched with things to do tonight. And, incidentally"— I gave a grimace—"we have a *dictée* at nine tomorrow morning, courtesy of Mme Tourdzie, remember?"

"Oh God, no! *C'est déguelasse!*" he said." Like most of us learning French, he liked to toss a few choice Gallic words about. "You know, Glynne, it's interesting. Why do you think Mme Tourdzie chooses something like André Gide's *The Counterfeiters* for dictations for us impoverished students? Maybe she figures we could pick up some tips."

I laughed. "I'll bet Tourdzie, being Tourdzie, will dictate those boring parts we skipped over."

A clock somewhere chimed the half-hour. Ned glanced at his watch. "Ten-thirty!" He looked at me, his eyes full of fun. "I'll be damned. I'd have thought nine-thirty. Still, on occasion I've been wrong!"

As he said the word "wrong," a low bubble of laughter seemed caught in his throat. I'd heard it before. Was it a tic? It was endearing, a quirk of which he seemed to be unaware.

We took the metro to Saint-Paul, my stop, and in a few minutes we were outside my building.

Ned propped one hand against the wall, holding my hand with the other.

"What fun this has been," I said.

"Oh, more than just fun." He paused. "I take it you're not going to ask me up for tea or anything?"

"You're right. It's late."

"You know, I want to meet little Cathy soon."

"Perhaps."

"Perhaps—is that your favorite word?"

"Perhaps."

He laughed, and I wondered if he would try to embrace me. Instead, he took my hand and pressed it to his lips. I nearly jumped, as though touched by a hot iron.

"*Bonsoir, Madame,*" he said, walking off with long strides toward the metro station. I fumbled with the doorknob, then stopped and turned to look back down the street. At the same moment he turned and saw me looking at him. We stayed staring at each other in the distance before he shouted something I couldn't hear. Then he waved and walked away.

Chapter Twenty-four

It was early October. A month had passed since I had dined at La Bonne Bouffe with Ned. We'd talked over coffee after class a few times, and one time he'd come for afternoon tea to our house. After that, Cathy was willing to be his slave, even though he had not allowed her to win at pick-up sticks, a game she rarely lost. When we had devoured his box of gorgeous cakes and Cathy was in the kitchen doing her homework, I asked him, "Couldn't you have let her win just once?"

He shook his head. "Absolutely not. It would be demeaning to her as well as to me." He warmed to the topic. "I'm an ardent game player. All kinds of games. Playing for high stakes still gets my blood going. The fact is, there are bags of money or other prizes to be won or lost. You call it gambling; I call it a game. I know a lot of people play purely for enjoyment. No chips, no money bets, nothing, right?"

"Right. That's how I play."

"And yet even with nothing at stake you feel delight, maybe even pride, in winning, and chagrin or disappointment when you've lost."

"Naturally."

"Well, it seems to me that if you play a game unfairly, by making false moves so your opponent can win, it denigrates not only the game but the players."

"But Cathy's only a child," I protested.

"I'll bet that kids who grow up to be sore losers are the ones who never lost any game when they were small. Their mothers saw to it that they always won."

"Okay, Ned. You win! I'll reconsider letting Cathy win in our next game of draughts or pick-up sticks. Not that I ever do win in pickup sticks—her tiny fingers move so well, she wins fairly."

He lit a Gauloise and inhaled with pleasure.

Then he set about fixing Mme Doucet's clock, an ornate object with cherubs and trumpets that had sat on the mantelpiece not telling the time for months. In fact, it may not have worked since the Napoleonic era. Joe had wanted to return it to Madame, but I liked it. Even if it were not a true antique, it was an *objet d'art* among our clutter.

I called Cathy in. "Now watch closely what Ned does to fix the broken clock," I said.

Ned added gravely, "It'll be mended or broken forever." He grasped the clock.

Cathy said anxiously, "*Maman*, what's he going to do?" Her eyes were wide.

"He's having a go at getting the clock to go tick-tock again, as clocks are meant to do."

We stared at him as he rolled up his shirt sleeves, then flung the clock almost to the ceiling. It fell with a heavy thud onto the carpet. I closed my eyes, picturing Mme Doucet's face were she to come in.

But next minute we were shrieking, "Ned, oh clever Ned. How did you do it?" Gently he placed the ticking clock in Cathy's hands.

"Stop asking silly questions, young lady. You saw with your own eyes how." He was grinning.

"But I don't understand. What happened, Ned?" I was as mystified as my daughter.

He shrugged. "Sometime a good knock can get things going." He turned to Cathy. "Now, it doesn't always work, so don't start flinging things about. Even I—and I'm a good thrower—sometimes make things worse." He beamed at me. "What else needs fixing?"

Cathy fell asleep before he left. At the door, his eyes held mine and then he slowly began planting kisses on my cheeks, then my lips, until at last I felt his tongue opening up my mouth. The stab of heat, first in my thighs, then permeating my entire body, was one I had missed, and I was about to respond when an awful reality intervened. Mme Doucet! I heard the sound of her plodding footsteps on the stairs. That bloody woman! If only she would turn into a pillar of salt.

I pulled away "Listen, Ned, My landlady is on her way in."

"Now?" He tried to sound cool, but his voice was hoarse.

We listened as a key began to rattle in the lock, and we both stepped backwards. Then we started laughing like teenagers.

As she opened the door, Madame's head twitched on seeing Ned, but she managed a thin smile. "I don't think we have met before, Monsieur." Then, addressing me, " I am sorry if I have arrived at an . . . inopportune moment." Did I detect a note of triumph in her voice?

"No, you came at the best of times," I said. "My friend was just leaving." I introduced him. On hearing that his name was Ned Shilling, her face came to life. "Really? *C'est extraordinaire!* You have the exact same name as the silver piece in *Grande Bretagne.*" She then plied him with a string of personal questions. He managed to be succinct without being rude in his answers until finally, unable to think up any more unsuitable questions, she bid us adieu and glided along the corridor in her snakelike walk toward her kitchen.

Ned whispered, "Is she still lurking about anywhere?" He peered around. "God! She's insatiable." He put his long arms around my waist and kissed me briefly on the lips. After shutting the door, he called through it, "I loved meeting Cathy. She's just grand."

I smiled and said "*D'accord*—"I agree," then, "See you in class tomorrow."

Lying in bed that night, I thought of an exchange I'd had with Joe months ago. We'd made love and I was dozing off when he shook my arm excitedly.

"Glynne, I've been thinking. All the aphrodisiacs in the world— the oysters, the perfumes, the music—can't make it happen. It's either there or it isn't."

"What do you mean by 'it'?" I had asked, my eyes wide in the dark.

"'It' is the beast in us."

I hadn't liked the image of the beast and was silent.

After a pause, he'd said. "Glynne, it's a beautiful, incomprehensible beast—one, thank heavens, we can't tame."

Now I thought about Ned. My physical attraction to him was undeniable. Yet I knew that, excited as I was, I probably would never fall in love with him, just as I had probably never fallen in love with Joe. And even though I hadn't made love with Ned yet, I sensed that this engaging and handsome companion was about to fall for me, and that it might become a problem. La Grande Colette would probably say, "Seize and savor the moment." I decided I would listen to her.

The next morning, the air was chill and damp. As I walked to the Sorbonne, a few brown leaves spiraled down from gray branches, to be whipped up again by sudden gusts of wind to hang suspended in shivering parabolas for a few seconds before descending. I watched this pantomime for a moment, wondering why I had never noticed it before.

On the boulevard Saint-Michel, the students' discussions had moved indoors, behind glass doors, where people argued over cups of steaming coffee. On the street, people trotted briskly, swinging briefcases or hugging piles of books to their chests. It seemed all at once that everyone in the 5th *arrondissement* was wearing a heavy hand-knit sweater coupled with a brightly colored wool scarf.

Cathy was wearing her white-and-blue hood-scarf. This small headgear had taken me an entire year to make, knitting and purling and dropping stitches. Yet despite the bunched bits sewn together, it made Cathy looked French and jaunty.

When we arrived at her school, I saw a crowd of parents clustering around a notice taped to the front door. "Can you beat that?" a blonde woman asked me as I approached.

"Probably not," I said agreeably, squeezing in to discover what the rumpus was all about. I saw four typewritten lines stating that an after-school play group would be available weekdays from three to five to all parents.

I almost shrieked with joy. Here it was on a silver platter, a gift of two extra hours a day: a chance to breathe, to argue and laugh with friends, to swap ideas, to wander into museums, art galleries, and churches, to putter about bookstores, to bike through every *arrondissement* in Paris. I could go to the movies and gaze up at Jean Gabin, smoldering in the dark. I could sit in Hemingway's leather chair at the Dôme among the painters, musicians, and writers. Ned, of course, might enter and watch as I bestowed a smile at a bearded artist whose dark-blue eyes burned into mine. *"Mon Dieu,"* he was saying *"Merci.* Thank God I've found you at last! You have the face and the body I have all my life searched for. I will pay you handsomely to be my model and—"

Then I stopped dead in my narcissistic charade. Little Cathy, poor darling. Where did she fit into all this? I thought of her face glowing with happiness as she raced to meet me at after school. How just doing whatever we did then—waiting at the butcher counter, buying a baguette at the *boulangerie,* going to the carousel or the Jardin du Luxembourg to watch the toy sailboats—just the two of us, really was fun and satisfying. Why in heaven's name was I even considering changing things? True, I was always on the run, everlastingly late for things, with brilliantly inventive excuses. Not to mention a to-do list the length of the Seine. Yet I was happy most of the time.

As though adding substance to this view, a man shouted hoarsely, "To arrive at nine and leave at five—non! My little Jean is not a factory worker yet."

I caught his eye and nodded guiltily.

"Speak for yourself, Monsieur," came a shrill rejoinder. "I bring my Charlotte each day, leaving twin babies back home waiting for me. And with it all, my husband wants a cooked dinner, starting with blood sausage every night of the week. So it will be an answer to my prayers."

The debate stopped when the school door opened and Mlle Brissard appeared. Dressed as always in a dark cardigan that revealed a light blouse beneath, and with a silvery pince-nez hanging from a cord on one side of a long dark skirt, she spoke clearly.

"Bonjour everybody. I am glad to observe your interest in the new after-school play group that is being formed. I wish to add that it is financed by the government, and so, like our little school, it will be entirely free of charge."

I stood there, thinking, "I am a selfish pig." I mulled over the best way to tell Cathy about the after-school play group in a way that would let me know if she wanted to be a part of it. First, I'd make sure she would never suspect how I longed for the extra two afternoon hours for myself. It might hurt her feelings. I'd use a matter-of-fact voice and talk about what was in the program: arts and crafts, games, dancing.

If she appeared overly enthusiastic I'd squelch things by telling her it would cut into our usual afternoon jaunts. I'd mention such favorite things as the paths at the Jardin du Luxumbourg, where she wheeled her wooden hoop with a stick, and the fun of going to the little shops choosing things for supper and chatting with the owners.

If her face fell or her eyes looked unhappy because she did not want to give this up, I'd back off fast and tell her how lucky we were to be able to choose. "We can say no to this play group. Why? Because we like what we're already doing more than any planned program."

If she appeared pensive or undecided, I'd suggest she try it out for a few days and see for herself. I didn't think she'd want to change the status quo. She relished routines. When I'd tell her a story I'd told her before, she listened for errors. "Mum! You forgot to growl when you said 'the bear.'" Once I'd added almonds to the yogurt and apricot jam we have for dessert. Grimacing, she'd spooned them onto her saucer. "Yes, I quite like almonds," she'd said, "but yogurt is best the way we always have it."

That afternoon when I picked her up from school, she seemed more than usually affectionate, running over to hurl herself at me. I decided this wasn't the time to bring up the after-school group. Instead, I swung her around by her arms, letting her shriek happily until the street began to whirl about me. Afterward, I told her a *pneu* had come to our house. She knew that *pneus* were thin blue letters sent by Parisians, delivered within two hours to any address in Paris. This complex system of tubes and air pumps solved the problem for hundreds of thousands of phoneless Parisians. It was a fast way to relay important news, make or break a rendezvous, or send happy wishes for a birthday, and it was very cheap.

We sat on the bench outside her school. "I'll read it to you," I said, taking it from my pocket. "It's from David and Tamara."

"Is Tamara going to have a baby?"

"Yes. It's just a tiny seed in her tummy now, but it grows a bit each day, and in about five or six months the seed will have become a little baby."

Cathy looked solemn. "When it turns into a baby, I want to be the babysitter. Can I?"

"Maybe," I said. I began to read the *pneu* aloud. "'We want to take you and Cathy this Saturday to a wonderful place called the Jardin d'Acclimatation. It's a big park in the Bois de Boulogne with sheep and goats who love to be petted, and there's a boat with room for four that glides along a narrow canal all the way around the park. There's a red train, too. From it you can see herds of ponies, and if you're lucky some white geese. When it picks up speed it makes a loud *choo-choo* and clouds of steam fly out of the chimney. So how about it? Be ready for a blast. We'll fetch you at 9 on Saturday. Big hugs from David and Tam.'"

"Oh Mum, I want to go. Say again what is that place jardin thing, acleem—what's it called?!"

"Jardin d'Acclimatation, but I can't go. I have to write my essay then. It's due on Monday." But Cathy's downcast face turned to joy when I told her that David and Tamara, whom she adored, would love to have her all to themselves.

"Poor Mum," she said. "Still, I'll tell you all about it." She rose and, humming, ran up the street before returning to hold my hand.

"*Maman*, listen please, and don't say no right away, because I know you will. Please wait before you say no. There's an after-school play group that we're going to have, and I really want to go. Paul, Chantal, Daphne, and Amalie will be going. *Maman*, it will be such fun. What do you think? Please say yes, or at least maybe."

I tried to look glum. "Well, perhaps. Probably yes, if you're so sure."

I've seen my daughter near ecstasy several times, but that afternoon she reached the stars.

Chapter Twenty-five

Ned and I were scurrying along the rue Soufflot after class on a cloudy October afternoon. It had stopped raining, and we wanted to get to Roland's Discothèque, a record shop, before the next downpour. The owner of the shop, M. Roland, a spidery figure with gentle eyes, never gave up on his mission to steer us toward French classical composers. In those days, record stores had listening booths so you could listen before buying. Only after we'd heard a recording of Saint-Saëns or Debussy would M.Roland produce a couple of more contemporary records for us to enjoy. We rarely if ever bought anything, and he never expected us to. He was amused by our enthusiasm and youth, although less so by our ignorance, and he wanted to teach us to appreciate the finest.

This time, when we entered the listening booth, we noticed that there was a record already on the turntable. I asked Ned to play it for a moment while we took off our jackets. Soon we were holding hands, swaying, loving every moment of the song. We felt a shared happiness with the singer, whoever he was, and with each other. And we could actually understand half the lyrics.

"Oh my Lord, *yeeoww!*" Ned yelled. He looked at the label. "The singer's name is Yves Montand. You know what, Glynne? I'll lay a bet this guy will go places."

We wondered where this genius of a singer came from. M. Roland said he himself had never listened to the record but had ordered it for a customer.

After that, Ned and I went to Roland's Discothèque just to listen to Yves Montand's records. Closeted in the booth, we'd wait with keen anticipation for the sudden break in Montand's voice—a sort of wobble between happiness and madness that made us moan with joy. Yves Montand was our special private discovery.

Then one day Ned and I were passing a kiosk and I stopped dead in astonishment. There was *our* Yves Montand on a large poster. He was holding a cigarette in two fingers while waving to us and every other passerby. His energy seemed to burst out of the poster, teeming with life force, his eyes twinkling impishly. Above the image was the announcement "L'Étoile à l'Étoile"—The Star at the Star Theatre—where he would be doing a one-man show for six weeks. In a second we were robbed of the notion that he was our own private discovery.

I was indignant. "But how could we have been so deranged?" I shouted, the cold drops stinging my cheeks. We eyed each other sheepishly. Then we began to laugh. What else was there to do? "Remember your grave prophecy," I said. "He'll go places!"

A few days later, Ned announced that he'd bought us tickets for the show. When I asked what they cost, he pushed out his lips and whistled."

I took his arm, saying, "How wonderfully clever of you."

"The tickets will recompense us for our delusions of grandeur," Ned said. And the concert will be our special memory forever."

Ned had the easy generosity of a gambler, and I loved that in him. When he'd won at pool or bridge, or whenever there was cash around, he was a happy spender. He immediately began planning our night at the Théâtre de L'Étoile, about four weeks hence. It had to be perfect. He'd cook a superb dinner, all ready for heating when we got back.

"And after we've wined and dined,"—here he'd paused delicately—"well, who's to know? Other remarkable things may happen."

Certainly it seemed possible. For once we'd be alone in his apartment, since he'd encouraged the couple he shared it with to visit Mont Saint-Michel, in Normandy, that weekend. And thanks to my dear friends Tamara and David, I wouldn't have to hurry home: they were thrilled to have Cathy to themselves for a couple of days. Best of all, in Ned's apartment there would be no chance of Mme Doucet's plodding footsteps interrupting us.

Part of Ned's determination to make this night perfect was that a few days after the show he'd be embarking on a serious work, long overdue: finishing his thesis "Lesser-Known Reasons for the French Revolution." He hadn't touched it for a while.

"So," he said, as we walked along arm in arm, "I will be retiring to my room with a dozen packs of Gauloises, a pot of coffee, a large bottle of scotch, and my typewriter. And, *bien sûr*, some baguettes and cheese. I'll go nowhere, see no one. And I won't welcome interruptions, except for one nice *pneu* from you. Make that two *pneus,* since it's you."

"How long will it take you to finish?"

"Two weeks, maybe longer."

"And school?" I asked, "You won't be coming to class?"

"Nope."

"And bridge? And Ping-Pong? How about pool?" I was just about to add, "And me?" but I didn't. I didn't want him to think I couldn't live without him. Nor did I want to give him false hopes about my feelings, which were mixed. Safe to say I found Ned terribly attractive as well as good company. But was that all?

I pondered the state of being in love. What was it actually? I'd thought I was in love with Joe when I was seventeen. My feelings had been inconstant and unpredictable, and in a few years they had changed. With Ned there was camaraderie, affection, and ardor—not so bad. Was anything missing? Wasn't being in love supposed to give your skin a special sheen, your looks a radiance? Yet I looked the way I always did. Maybe I should try harder, not hold back my feelings. But if I had to try so hard, didn't that say something, too?

Ned, of course, was not privy to these goings-on. He gave me one of his smiles where the left lip seemed higher than the right. "Anyway, my love, you'll be taking notes in class for the two of us during that time."

Soon we were installed at Dupont's, across the street from the Sorbonne, enjoying *café crèmes*. Our fingers met across the table, and then, in an unusual public display, he reached over and kissed the inside of my wrist.

Then he began talking about his mother. "She weighs at most a hundred pounds, but she's tough. She had to be, since my dad was a farmer. She was a schoolteacher when they met. English was her

subject. Back then, that meant penmanship, spelling, and grammar. About ten years ago, when my father died and I'd turned
thirteen, she was advised to sell the farm. But she refused. She
hired a daily hand to help and managed to make a success of it.
She's still farming today."

"Do you have a photo of her?" I asked.

He took out his wallet. "It's somewhat ragged and two years old,
but you'll get an idea."

I studied it. "Not much like you, except for the blonde hair.
She's really pretty. And she looks determined."

"I'm more like my old man." He smiled. "I was often described
as gangly as a boy."

He told me how his mother was known for her baking. "It was
sold at all the church functions, and the whole congregation would
make a rush for her pies." He paused. "You know, Glynne, you'd
like her. The two of you would get on like a house on fire."

But how does a house on fire get on? I thought. It burns to the
ground, or it smolders and smells forever. "Think so?" I said.

"Well, remember, she lives a cloistered life. We're two miles
from the nearest neighbor. She's only once in her life been outside
of Indiana. I mean she's never met a Jew in her life, let alone an
English-Egyptian one."

I took a sip of coffee to hide my reaction. Never met a Jew in
her life? Somehow it brought to mind a friend who had traveled
to India to see the greater one-horned rhino.

I said, "I can't put my finger on it, but I'm appalled by what you
just said."

The color drained from his face. "Glynne! How can you be appalled? I was telling you a fact."

Seeing the expression on my face, he added, "Please don't be
sore. There's nothing to feel hurt about. Do you think I'd deliberately say something to cause you pain? I was trying to say that my
mother is a simple person with strengths as well as weaknesses."

Had my feelings toward him altered ever so subtly, or would
this blow over? Anyway, I was late picking up Cathy, and I rushed
off to fetch her from her still-new afternoon play program, which
she loved even more than school.

Chapter Twenty-six

David arrived promptly on Saturday morning to take Cathy. I hugged her and said, "*Sois sage*"—"Be good."). David told me I'd be missing Tamara's home-made clafouti and I said, "Well, you can always bring me a consolation serving when you return with Cathy."

David said, "Maybe there won't be any leftovers." He winked at Cathy, and taking her eager hand, he left me to my coffee.

I dressed for a day at home in a faded tartan skirt that was too tight to go out in topped by a hand-knit sweater I'd bought at the Marché aux Puces, or flea market. The neckline had squares that alternated up and down, like crenellations on a fortress. I'd only paid the equivalent of a dollar-fifty for it.

Mme Doucet had left for a few days to be with her daughter, who was recovering from an appendectomy. With Cathy gone as well, I was soon absorbed by a story I was reading by Guy de Maupassant called "*Boule de suif*"—"Ball of Fat." It's the tale of a prostitute who is round and chubby and who travels with "respectable" people by coach on a long journey during the Franco-Prussian War. They shun her and exclude her from their conversation until she pulls out a basket of cold roast chicken, *paté*, bread, cheese, and wine. The greed and unconcealed opportunism of the "noble" group in contrast to the generous nature of the simple woman is at the heart of the story. I began writing my essay and was totally engaged.

The doorbell rang. I groaned. It certainly was not Ned; he never came round unexpectedly. Besides, I was meeting him later for the Yves Montand concert. I pulled open the heavy door and saw Théo framed in the doorway. I hadn't seen him for several weeks.

He gave a brusque laugh. "At last, Glynne. You've forgotten who I am, I think." It was a statement, not a question.

I was tempted to say, "I wish you'd forget about me." Instead I said, "Hello, Théo. You look well. Come in." He looked as if had showered; his hair was slicked back and his face ruddy. "Actually, right now I'm terribly busy," I added.

"I came to give Madame her injection. Afterwards, I'll examine Cathy."

"They're not here. Friends have taken Cathy out for the day, and Madame is with her daughter."

"So you have no one here today," he said, following me into the sitting room. He lowered himself into the armchair and I sat opposite him on the couch.

"Theo, the fact is, I'm desperately writing—"

"Writing what?" he interrupted.

"A paper on Guy de Maupassant's story '*Boule de suif*.'"

"It is an excellent story."

"*C'est formidable*," I said, smiling. "But look, I'm rushed. It's turning out to take longer than I thought. I felt his eyes on me. He was staring openly at my breasts.

To distract him, I asked, "How's it going with your work?"

He shrugged. "There are armies of sick people. Things you can't even imagine."

"But don't you feel a satisfaction in helping them?"

"Don't patronize me, Glynne."

"What do you mean, patronize you? Why are you acting like this?"

He rose unexpectedly and suddenly was towering over me. I noticed the movement of his Adam's apple quivering above the neck of his blue sweater. He began to shout, his words ricocheting like bullets. "You don't admit it, but you want me the way I want you. You've wanted me from the first." He grabbed my hand.

I pulled it back swiftly. "You're wrong," I said in the quietest voice I could muster. "I like you, and I appreciate your taking care of Cathy. But I do *not* want you. Nor have I ever had any such feelings toward you."

His eyes spat anger. "We'll soon see."

He dragged me from the chair onto the floor. I managed to get up and headed for the doorway, but he grabbed one of my arms in a steely grip and dragged me back into the room. He pushed me down. I fought hard, and I was strong for my weight, but he was stronger, and, breathing heavily, he smothered me like a lead blanket. He pinned one of my hands on the carpet with his knee. I swung my free fist at his face with all my strength; it landed on his neck and he grunted. If only I could kick him, but I couldn't get either leg out from under his body, which was crushing me painfully.

"Stop! Pig!" I screamed. I looked up and saw his crimson face and demented eyes boring into me. How could I escape? "Théo," I said in a low voice, "don't be crazy."

He was pulling up my skirt. "I am crazy—for you. You want me. You're going to get it."

Until that moment, I had believed rape to be impossible if a man was unarmed. But here was Théo now, panting, his fly unbuttoned, his full weight on me. His wrist had slid so that it pressed deep into my mouth and against my nose. I couldn't breathe. I tried to bite his arm. Almost at the end of my strength, I wriggled my hips, the one part of me that wasn't jammed tight between the floor and him. Then there was the horror of feeling him entering. He climaxed in seconds and fell back, moaning and gasping. I closed my eyes.

When I opened them, he reached out his hand to help me up. I ignored it. There were tears rolling down his face as I slowly rose to sit on the couch. He knelt at my knees. "Glynne, please accept to marry with me."

Would this nightmare never end? I felt sick to my stomach and knew I might soon vomit.

"Get up, Théo," I said evenly. I pointed to the couch. Sheepishly he rose, sat down, and smoothed his clothes. "I'll be back" I said. I went to the bathroom to throw up. I returned with two glasses of water.

"You violated me." I heard the tremble in my voice; I couldn't control it. "For committing rape you could be locked away for years." Even as I said this I doubted it. Who would be my witness?

"Rape is not a big crime in France," he said. "A woman sometimes submits, that is all." He put his arm across his eyes for a few seconds. "Believe me, I did what I did because I really thought you wanted me to."

"No. Never."

"Glynne, please. I want to marry with you."

I threw him a look of hatred.

His head dropped to his chest. Then I heard him sob, giant strangled things rising from some deep abyss. I remembered Joe telling me how when Théo was in Dachau at the age of eleven he had been held down, screaming, and forced to witness his parents being shot.

I thought to put an arm around him, but he'd already calmed down. He pulled a cotton handkerchief from his pocket and loudly blew his nose. He spoke in a voice thick with sadness. "I thought you liked me too but didn't want to admit it." He groaned. "I didn't come on purpose to do this. It was like a fire in me, I couldn't stop. I swear on my dead parents' heads this will never happen again."

"It certainly won't because I'm never going to see you again."

"Glynne," he coaxed, "you know I am a good teacher. Perhaps we can continue with *Madame Bovary* sometime?"

"I think not."

"But please, do you forgive me?"

"Théo, you forced yourself on me. I can't excuse you just because you had a rotten childhood. Please go."

He nodded and stood up.

"And please understand, now and forever, I am not, nor ever will be, interested in you as a lover."

"I understand," he said, shuffling off toward the door.

I tried for a lighthearted touch and called after him, "Next time, don't rape the woman you want to marry."

He had the grace to accept the joke and looked back at me with a pained smile.

I sat without moving for a long time, enveloped in a thick gray pall. I talked to myself. I am alive, I have good brains and a body, I have a loving family and wonderful friends. I have a child who is the sun, moon, and stars to me. Be content. What took place is unchangeable. Then I thought, I must douche.

I went to the bathroom and did a thorough job. Then I sat on the wooden stool near the tub, half crying, still talking to myself. Don't act like a self-pitying booby. Reserve some of your pity for that blighted orphan who saw his father murdered, then his mother. My trauma will fade, little by little. Eventually it will heal. Already it's a little in the past.

But why had Théo thought I wanted him? My mind cascaded back, reaching for something. Then I remembered the time Joe had asked him to dinner, how his pointy shoe had found mine under the table. I hadn't pulled my foot away instantly. In fact, I'd felt a momentary thrill.

How glad I was to be seeing easy-going Ned tonight! And soon to be at the theatre watching Yves Montand, that appealing singer whose politics were ours, whose songs were alive in our heads. I vowed to myself never to tell Ned or anyone else about this sad, ugly story. I was done talking about it to myself, too. It was time to get up and make myself a strong cup of tea. After which I'd take a bath and wash my hair so it would be shining before I left the house.

Chapter Twenty-seven

Who could have possibly known that our big night would be taking place after that ghastly morning with Théo? I met Ned at a small café near the theatre for a glass of wine, and we arrived at the theatre to find the place jam-packed with people of all types, from workers in woolen sweaters and slouch caps to well-dressed couples in the best seats near the orchestra. Where we were, on high, it was crowded with students like us, thrilled at the chance to see this left-wing supporter of labor unions in performance.

Stumbling across a railroad of legs, my hand in Ned's, we eventually reached our seats and flopped down in them. Joy! They were nearly center stage.

Ned turned to me and asked, "How's your seat? Will you be able to see everything?"

I craned my neck slightly, trying to see over a woman's hat. "Yes, mostly."

Ned then slipped off his jacket, folded it, and told me to sit on it. Now I could see. I thought, okay, Ned is not perfect, but he's so thoughtful about my needs and comfort and hardly concerned with his own.

"That's better, isn't it?"

"It's perfect. When Yves comes on stage, I'll be able to see his toes." Which, it turned out, would be a big plus for the final song.

Ned held up the playbill for us both to read. I studied it, but something strange was happening. I couldn't make it out. The letters were so faded as to be unreadable. I scowled and blinked, peering close to see and swiftly recoiled. Slowly I took another look. Théo's haggard face was staring back at me. I shivered, and fear sliced across me. I closed my eyes tightly but could hear his voice, that importunate cry, "I thought you wanted me, too."

I stifled a gasp. Ned's warm fingers covered mine as he leaned across to murmur something in my ear. As he bent toward me, I saw the program—with Théo's picture on it—fall to the floor. I felt relieved. Observing the row after row of heads in front of me was also comforting. I was, after all, with an appealing man in a theatre crowded with people just like us, ready to be entertained by a fantastically talented young man whose songs gave us all delight. All that was needed was to sit back and take it in.

And now the heavy green curtain was starting to go up. The stage stood empty for a few seconds, then Montand ran to its center. He was wearing an open-necked white shirt and dark pants. His fans simply wouldn't stop applauding, shouting, whistling, and stamping. He held up his hands and there was instant silence.

"Okay," he said. "*Ça va?*"—"How are things?" His voice was vibrant, male, and Gallic.

The crowd roared back, "*Ça va bien.*"

Yves grinned. "*Moi, aussi, pas trop mal.*"— "Me too, not bad." Before they could start clapping again, he casually hummed "*Lala la la laaa lala la la laaa.*" The piano player picked up the melody, and Montand began singing "*Un Gamin de Paris*"—"A Parisian Urchin." The song was already a hit, and the audience stamped their feet approvingly.

Ned and I exchanged quick looks. We had reeled with pleasure hearing this song in the record store a few weeks ago, but here onstage Montand went even further. He inhabited the song. He was the cheeky little newsboy, mischievous but filled with childish pride; he was the dancer, too, the clickety-clack of his shoes tapping out the rhythm. And, of course, he was the singer, the star, his hands and body gracefully telling the story.

He kept up a rapid pace, one song following another, providing a variety of selections evoking different moods. Listening, I felt at one with the audience, and with Ned, too, all of us caught up in his web. I forgot about the program with Théo's picture in it or not.

Montand was a fantastic performer, and the audience responded to the changes in the mood of the songs. From being crazy with delight with one, we were saddened with the next, or convulsed with laughter by another. He could also be very funny. Some-times, like excitable children, the audience couldn't allow it when he reached the last word of a song. They refused to let it end. Ned and I shouted along with them. "*Bis! Bis!*"—"Again! Again!"

Montand would disappear into the wings, only to come out singing the last verse of the song, sometimes more than once. For nearly two hours our eyes were glued on him. Once or twice, Ned played with my hand, but he let it fall gently; we were both so absorbed by the show. One song, "*À Paris,*" made me laugh and cry simultaneously. It made me ache for what I loved about Paris: couples arm-in-arm, the sounds of church bells, the cheeky news-paper boys shouting out the headlines, the smells, the Seine. In fact, listening to it made me feel homesick for a city in which I was still living. I wanted to hear this song whenever I had the urge and decided I'd actually buy it instead of trotting to the old music shop to listen.

The final song was "*Une Demoiselle sur une balançoire*"—"A Girl on a Swing." The music's simple phrases, played crisply on the piano, sounded almost like Bach, and its ending, a few notes running down the scale, seemed unbearably beautiful. Montand sang the words distinctly, ending the first two lines with an up-ward *uh* sound, which gave the lyrics a slangy intensity. The song was about a beautiful girl on a swing and as she rose and fell, you could see her lovely white legs under her black skirt.

Somehow, Montand was that girl on the swing, high above the world below, enjoying the pleasure of the movement, but he was the observant watcher, too. However, he did it with an air of non-chalant curiosity rather than a voyeur's prurience. The tune held strong, and the manner in which he sang—head flung back, then falling to one side—left one longing for the nearest park just to see a girl on a swing.

Having sung two encores of the song, at last he stood, breathing hard in front of us, charmingly disheveled. "*Eh bien*, this time you and me together. We'll sing the first verse only, twice. And if you can't remember the words, just hum *la la la la*, as if you were sing-ing to a baby." The audience laughed. He continued, "After we've sung it twice—and I expect to hear you sing loudly—I want to be deafened." He grinned. "Do you think you can manage?"

The audience yelled back, "Yes!"

"Afterwards, we'll have to say goodnight." A quiet fell over the theatre. "I hope it has been as good a night, and as happy a one for you as it has for me."

The music started, and a loud chorus of men's deep baritones, harmonizing with the softer tones of the women, filled the air. At once, everybody was singing about the beautiful girl on the swing. I remembered how shy English audiences could be when invited to join in. Half-singing, but mostly listening, I knew I would never forget this moment.

I had to admit that a girl on a swing enjoying herself, unaware of her white legs beneath her black skirt, was not a high-minded theme. Yet with all the voices rising and falling, it sounded totally majestic. I'd been able, at least for a while, to put behind me the abject misery of what had taken place that morning.

When the singing ended there was silence, soon broken by Montand energetically clapping and bowing his head in appreciation. "*Vous étiez superbe,*" he said—and we were, too. I wanted to shout "Hear, hear!" but of course I kept my English tongue still. Everyone cheered "our" Yves: "Bravo, Bravo!" And finally, the end: Yves waving a nonchalant hand at the audience as he tap-danced into the wings, rendering "*Une Demoiselle*" with his feet alone, clickety-clicking across the stage. The clapping only died down when the lights came on, and people pulled themselves into their coats and headed for the exits. As I was getting into my jacket, a blonde woman in black near me got to her feet and looking in my direction said breathlessly, "*Mais il etait du tonnerre, ce type.*" He was terrific (thunder), this guy.

Her eyes were luminous. She seemed to be all alone. I smiled back, saying "*Ah oui, ah oui, ah oui.*" I'd liked to have added, "and lightning, too," but couldn't summon the word: "*éclair?*" "*l'electricite?*" Whatever I said might bring on that scrunched expression of French disdain, or even worse, the over-polite "*Comment?*" Explain. So I settled for "*Il est vraiment fort*" (he's really great), which started her off again, "*Ah oui, ah oui, ah oui,*" she purred, nodding with conviction, "*Il est vraiment fort.*"

Ned was pulling at my arm, "Come on, Glynne, come on." I raised my brows and shook my head in apology at her, rolling my eyes to indicate "*Les hommes! Vous savez!*" Men! She smiled understandingly and waved a gloved hand at me.

Outside in the street, the atmosphere was lively. People hummed, lovers kissed, and for a few seconds Ned held me close. Then he stopped to light up a Gauloise, half closing his eyes as he took in a couple of long drags. "Fantastic," he said, as we walked along slowly.

Then, abruptly, holding the cigarette, its red end bright in the darkness, he began to twirl around and around, dangerously fast. I watched open-mouthed as his shoulder grazed a lamppost. Next thing he was running into the street hailing a cab.

"*Allons*, kid. Would you like a taxi ride?" He steered me toward the waiting cab.

As we drove off, I said, "Do you have enough money to pay for it?"

"I think so. I had a very nice game of pool last night." He sounded smug.

Ned and I sped through the streets of Paris, his arm around my shoulders. When the cab stopped, the driver, a large man with a scarlet nose, said, "*Eh voilà! On est là , Mademoiselle et Monsieur.*" Ned gave him some bills, and the driver beamed at him before driving off, turning his head once to shout, "*Merci monsieur, et bonsoir.*"

Chapter Twenty-eight

I was seeing Ned's flat in the 14th *arrondissement* for the first time. His newly married friends, Andrew and Meg, who'd rented it for a year, had let out a room to him.

Ned showed me around hurriedly. "I've got things to do in the kitchen. The paint on the walls is still drying, so don't touch! My friends painted it themselves. I'll bet you won't like the color. It wouldn't be my choice, either, but it's their space. And they've worked on it like beavers for days."

"Like dark-brown beavers," I couldn't resist adding, for the walls throughout were an unadulterated mud brown. It occurred to me that they must have scoured Paris to find such a color.

"So now"—Ned waved his arm in the air—"look around all you want, and work up a voracious appetite. A memorable din-dins, we hope, is on its way." He squeezed my shoulder, then dove for the kitchen.

I walked around the apartment. It had a small dining room, the usual inefficient Parisian kitchen, a living room, and two bedrooms. All that space and all so unappealing. In the dining room one lonely picture hung on a wall. It showed twisted dark trees with bats or moles penciled over the paint, all in the favored color. Unframed and unsigned, it wasn't hard to guess its creators. Andrew had done the trees, and Meg added the bats and/or moles in a spirit of whimsy. Or vice versa.

But perhaps I was missing the meaning of this weird picture?. Suppose one day, it became as famous as a Max Ernest, or a Braque, and I'd sneeringly dismissed it? Maybe a museum docent would describe it as an important protest to the American Pollyana culture of "happy ever afterism."

I suspected Meg would heartily dislike me. I would be dismissed as a good-time Charlie girl. Yet I had often been drawn to misanthropes like her and Andrew. Those few mute people who at parties strayed away from the stories and jokes in search of solitude. I often chased after them, eager for their life stories or to learn why they attended parties if they were seeking solitude. It usually turned out they were not meditating. They'd left the main stream simply because they didn't fit in. They yearned, in vain, to know the secret of conversation and wit and how to get on with people.

Meanwhile, good smells were emanating from the kitchen—spicy, meaty, fruity, winy aromas. Could one get as sloshed from meat and vegetables soaked in wine as from drinking glasses of wine? Ned would surely know.

What was going on in the kitchen, anyway? He was making enough noise for three. Also noises. I could identify the thump of heavy pots being shoved about on the stove and even recognized the oven door, which had the same feature as mine: whining when opened, clanging hard when shut. There was the continual opening and banging shut of cupboard doors, and a recurring beat, likely a whisk in a ceramic bowl. Suddenly, above all the racket, Ned began to sing, keeping time with the whisk. It was a great song.

I wandered into the kitchen and Ned pretended to scowl. "What the devil—why are you here? It's a surprise dinner, remember?"

His blond hair was tumbled over his forehead, his normally pale cheeks were flushed, and his shirt was rumpled. Gone was the calm and classic Ned I knew. Facing me was *monsieur le chef.*

"Okay." I said. "But what a dandy song. Will you sing it again? Then I'll go. I'll even turn my back now so I won't see what you're doing."

"Everything has been ready since this morning. I'm just doing last-minute touches," he said, and then began singing the wild song again, begging someone to "come on-a my house." He'd give the person candy, or a plum, or an apricot. Ned stopped singing. "That's all I know. Now buzz off." He shoved a copper candlestick into my hands. "Matches and candle are on the table. Dinner will be served in five minutes."

We ate very well, and finally both of us were in his bed. His face was over mine, one arm propped up supporting his weight while his hand slid slowly down my body and back up again. He spoke in a low voice, breathing fast. "I guess I must sound like every guy in your life, but God"—his hand was now pressing into the curve of my waist— "you've got a fantastic body."

I resisted saying, "The only thing wrong is my breasts are too big," though I was learning that for most men, no such phenomenon existed.

He was stroking and circling my shoulder blade while looking into my eyes. He said softly, his hand now cupping my shoulder, "Do you want to know when I first fell for you?"

I thought he'd say it was when he'd first kissed me.

"It was the first time I saw you striding in late to Mme Tourdzie's class. Do you remember giving me an unforgettable smile, for no reason at all, as though we were accomplices? Of course you don't." He paused. "It was before I knew you were always late."

"Always? *Tu exagères, chéri.*"

His reply was to nuzzle my neck, followed by a kiss. I wanted to respond but I couldn't. Had I been such a pig at dinner that I was too stuffed to want to make love? No, it couldn't be that. Joe and I had sometimes fallen into bed with full stomachs and we'd managed fine. Still, I'd drunk a lot of wine that night, sipping steadily along with each course, half-aware of Ned's agility in refilling the glasses. As Shakespeare says of drink in *Macbeth*, "it provokes the desire but takes away the performance." Though all of the wine Ned had downed seemed to have increased his desire, and it looked as though his performance wouldn't be at all diminished.

"At last, I've got you where you belong," he said, looking happily down at me.

No, I don't think so, I said to myself.

I tried hard to concentrate on him and work up some intensity to match his. But it was hopeless. My body seemed to crave calm and peace. My receptive zones were being unreceptive. Nothing he did seemed to get them stirring. He was indeed inventive, but after a while I wished he'd stop trying so hard.

He rolled over on his back, holding my waist tightly, so that I was lying on top of him. He wasn't going to give up so easily. His tongue tasted warm and sweet as it explored my mouth. Had it been any night other than this—twelve hours after Théo's hateful visit—I'd have willingly reciprocated.

Even if I wasn't in love with Ned, I found him attractive. I'd begun to doubt what being in love actually meant. I'd read hundreds of novels about love, but had I ever fully experienced it? One thing was sure: this tall man on whose body I was comfortably lying did not want peace and calm tonight.

Oh dear, I thought, *the perfect evening he'd envisioned wasn't likely to take place.* I could bluster my way out of it by saying I had a headache or an upset stomach. The latter was barely credible, since I'd not only made a clean sweep of a huge bowl of his *boeuf à l'ancienne* but had eaten two rich *coquilles St.-Jacques* for starters.

Finally I blurted, "Ned, I think it's not going to work. Somehow I'm not in the mood. I can't explain. Maybe I drank too much. Anyway, I'm sorry, but I just can't."

There was a long silence. Some part of me wanted to let go, let it all out, tell him about my morning with Théo, but I was scared to relive the horror of it so soon. I needed time to put it behind me. I might tell him later. Ned gave me one of his loveliest smiles. "You're just teasing me, you wicked witch."

Oh, Lord, how I wished I were. "I'm not," I said quietly. I stopped myself from adding "Guide's honor."

"I'm ashamed to be spoiling our perfect evening, especially after such an amazing dinner. But my body's acting weirdly."

It was, too. With Joe I'd responded quickly when being caressed. Now I couldn't even summon my own erotic fantasies. The feel of Ned's hands was giving me the sensation of a clumsy Swedish massage. Whatever I did, I knew the sex would be a fiasco. I suppose I could have faked all my responses, even to shrieking at a pretended climax. A friend had said it made everybody happy. *Hmm*, I thought, *not quite everybody.*

I took his hand and laid it on the pillow, my hand on top of his. Beneath me, his lean white chest was smooth and beautiful. "You have a lovely body, too" I said.

Then he said, with his Indiana accent, *"Glynne, ma chérie, que'est-ce que tu as?"*—"Darling, what's the matter?"

My voice was small when I spoke. "Actually, I'm sick about something that happened this morning. It's why I can't be responsive now."

"For God's sake, Glynne, what's up?"

"I'm sorry," I said, trying not to cry. I reached for his hand.

He began to stroke my head with his other. "Darling, tell me."

Théo's burning gaze as he'd stared at my too-tight skirt; my fury as the steely arms grabbed me; the abject remorse on his wet face afterward—I told Ned everything, even how I'd once played a little footsie with him under the table. That made me cry all the more.

"Jesus, baby, cry all you want. I'm here." Ned continued to stroke my head. "But you know, in a way you're lucky. Théo in his state could have left you with some broken bones. Sweetheart, listen to me. You'll be okay soon. It was hideous and ghastly, but it's over. For Théo it's another story. He'll be desperate. What he'll do next God only knows."

I started to tremble. Without further talk, Ned's arms and legs were around me, his warmth surrounding me. On and on I cried. He brought me some cold water. After I took a few sips, he washed my face with a cloth.

"Okay, honey. Here's the program for tonight," he said. "I'm going to read aloud from the book you lent me, Colette's *La Vagabonde*. You are allowed to fall into a languorous sleep mid-sentence. And you know what? That would be just fine. You needed to let it out. Tomorrow you'll awaken feeling much better. Wanna bet?"

"No bets with you. You always win," I said, gulping.

"Sweetheart, I know you pretty well. You're not a person who's going to dwell on sordid things too long. A shrink would say you need treatment to get things sorted out, but I know you'll soon be fine."

Unexpectedly, I smiled. "What a dear, dear man you really are!"

"You know, I've been trying to tell you this all along," he said.

I did fall asleep while he read. When I awoke and looked at my watch, I realized I'd slept nonstop for nine full hours.

I found Ned in the living room. "Ned, darling, I'm me again, and—

A steamer trunk half-filled with books and papers lay open in the middle of the room. He greeted me tensely.

"Heavens! What's happened, Ned?"

"Some bad news while you were in the arms of Morpheus. I'm returning to the States on Wednesday. I have two days to get all my stuff together."

"Why?" My mouth was dry.

"This morning I got a telegram from my Uncle Matthew, my mother's brother. My mother's in the hospital. A busted hip, plus other injuries. They want me to come home immediately." He shook his head. "Why the hell she climbs up that goddamn ladder in the barn beats me."

I hugged him tightly. "Oh! What a miserable thing to happen to her. But she'll be so happy to see you."

"The thing is, there's just me and my uncle. Likely I'll be taking over the farm for a while. Lord knows how long for."

I smiled but my stomach wrenched, knowing he'd no longer be in Paris, perhaps forever. I tried to picture living without his humor, fun, and companionship. How I'd miss that gleam of triumph in his eyes when he'd won at pool, and the follow-up: "Okay, kid. Wanna go out big tonight?" And Cathy, who had become his darling. No more sitting astride his shoulders or having her private carpenter to make toys or tell "trick" stories where he'd read a funny tale in a deadpan way to make her giggle or rides through Paris streets on his bike. How would I tell her?

We had not become lovers, and I hadn't fallen in love with him. Yet his friendship had become sewn into the fabric of my life in Paris. Before I left his house that morning I promised to see him off at the Gare du Nord in two days, when he'd take the train to Calais and from there the steamboat that crossed the ocean.

He told me he'd send a *pneu* with the day, time, and platform number. "And Glynne, it's not like when you go to Mme Tourdzie's class! Come late and you'll miss the train. And me!"

"I won't miss your train. In fact, let's both try to be early so we can have some time together before you leave."

Taking my hand in his, he walked me to the front door. We hung onto each other while he stroked my hair in an absent-minded way. It reminded me of how, when I was upset, I'd caress my cat, Charlotte, on my lap, focusing not on her but on myself, planning what my next move would be.

I looked up at him. "Ned, I have a hunch it will work out okay. I know it will." Then I opened the door and strode off to pick up Cathy.

Chapter Twenty-nine

Cathy wiped the remnants of an omelet of fried brains off her plate with a crust of baguette. "*Voilà*," she said. "All gone."

"People in America hardly ever eat brains," I told her. "Except the brainy ones."

She giggled uncertainly. "Well, anyway, I like the egg part more than the brains. I think eating them makes you a teeny bit more clever, don't you?"

"Maybe a teeny weeny-weeny bit. Since they are very nourishing."

"I know, but *maman*"—she leaped from the table—"we have to leave right now. I don't want to miss him."

The previous day Ned had insisted on having a farewell chat with Cathy. He told her he'd telephone her at six tonight at Roget's, the *bar-tabac* across our street.

We now scurried down our four flights of steps, crossed the street, and entered the dimly lit bar, where I sometimes took coffee. It was filled with regulars from the neighborhood. At that hour, it was standard practice for working men—and an increasing number of women—to take a cognac or an aperitif along with a cigarette to revive themselves before going home to dinner.

From behind the bar, M. Roget called out, "*Bonsoir Madame— et la petite aussi.*" What can I get for you?"

"Nothing to eat or drink tonight, thank you, *monsieur*. We're waiting for a telephone call that's coming on your phone downstairs at six. Is that okay?"

"*Mais oui, certainement.* No need to ask."

We walked down the narrow steps carefully. Once in the basement, we went to the back and opened the glass door that divided the telephone from the toilet. Cathy, tense with excitement, was hopping from one foot to the other.

At six precisely the phone rang. She screamed with joy, "*Le voici!*"—"Here he is!" Her eyes glowed. She pressed the earpiece tightly against her head so as not to miss a word. "*Bonsoir,* Ned. Hello."

Whereas adults had to bend low to talk into the metal mouthpiece on the wall, Cathy was standing on her tiptoes. Ned seemed to be asking her questions, as she just kept nodding into the mouthpiece. Then she smile shyly. She looked at me, her mouth open, before answering, "Yes, *Maman* is here. I can hear you. Ned! You sound so real, just the way you speak all the time. Are you hiding nearby? Can you hear me?"

She suddenly fell silent, looking flustered, gazing up as though for inspiration. She made a French pout, scowled, then smiled. "Yes, it is funny. But, Ned, I can't think what to say." After a glance at me, she said, "*Maman* said you'll eat dinner on the moving train tomorrow." She grinned conspiratorially. "So don't spill soup on yourself!"

His reply made her giggle helplessly. Then her face was solemn. "*Eh bien, Ned. Tu me manqueras.*"—I'll miss you." She started to cry, then shook her head. "You can't see me, but I'm sending you a big kiss." She smacked her lips on her hand and blew the kiss into the mouthpiece. I caught the unique gurgle in his voice as he responded, and then the sound of his answering kiss.

After we'd climbed back up to our apartment, we were both quiet. Cathy was pulling faces, often a sign of tears being held back. I got her into her pajamas right away and into bed and was getting down a favorite book, *Madame Souris—Mrs. Mouse*—to read with her, when she suddenly began to howl. "Oh *Maman!*" she cried, and flung herself out of bed, her arms about my legs, weeping as though she'd never stop. I picked her up and put her on my lap, where she had a good cry.

When her sobs had subsided, she raised a tear-stained face, and after a last quiver and gulp she said, "I don't like it when people you are used to just go away. Why do people have to leave? It's not fair!"

I stroked her forehead. There wasn't any answer. First Colin and Audrey and Ginger had left. Then Joe. And now Ned. "Cathy, darling, when you love someone and they have to leave, they're still with you in some ways, because you carry them in your heart until you see them again. In Ned's case, he simply must leave because his mother's had a very bad fall. She used to manage a big farm all by herself. Now she can't even feed the chickens or the pigs or stack the hay. So he has to go home and pitch in."

"But he really loves Paris. And he told me he loved us, me and you, as well."

"But Ned has with a mother who's in pain and who needs him."

She thought about this, then spoke in a small voice. "He'd be bad, I suppose, not to help his mother."

I nodded. "So how did you like your very first time talking on the telephone?"

"I heard him so clearly. I kept thinking he might be hiding somewhere and he'd jump up suddenly and say 'surprise!'"

Not much later, she was bouncing up and down on her bed and falling down with a thud, until I warned her that if she continued, Mme Doucet would be gliding in to check the bedsprings. Cathy lay down, breathless, and said, "Now Mum, you promised. *Madame Souris! Madame Souris!*"

I read until I noticed there'd been no interruptions for a while and saw that she was asleep. Her body seemed so small, her outline barely visible under the covers. I'd have liked to slip in beside her and snuggle up. But homework, laundry, and tomorrow's early rising stopped me.

I was awakened the next morning by an odd sensation about my ears. Cathy was astride my stomach, pulling my ear lobes.

"Hey, you," I shouted. "Stop! What do you think you're doing?"

She dropped her hands and, still sitting on me, asked in a dulcet voice, "Did you sleep well, *Maman?*"

"Very well. But not quite long enough." I shook my head. "I dreamed somebody was tugging my ears off. Do you imagine you could sleep while someone's pinching *your* ears? Whatever gave you that preposterous idea?"

She was jubilant. "Ned said to do it. He said it to me on the phone." She added importantly, "On the telephone, he said to wake you because he didn't want you to be late at the Gare du Nord."

My alarm suddenly buzzed its imperative peal. It was six, nearly daylight.

"But Cathy," I said. "Why did you wake me by pulling my ears? Why didn't you just shake me or give a shout?"

"It was you! Remember, you told me never to startle anybody who was sleeping. Remember, *Maman*?"

"Aren't you my clever poppet! You are perfectly and absolutely right."

She shot me such a gleeful smile that I never brought up the puzzling matter of why pulling the ears would be any less disturbing than giving a shout.

Chapter Thirty

Getting from my metro station, Saint-Paul, to the Gare du Nord, in the 10th *arrondissement*, was not a direct route. It involved a *correspondence*, or change, at République, that labyrinthine underground maze that connected a swarm of lines. Oh heavens! Had I missed a crucial sign to the Gare du Nord while hurrying through those tunnels and up and down the seemingly endless flights of stairs? Clueless and unsure whether to turn left or right, all the while envisioning Ned's indignant face, I took a left turn, my heart thumping with the sound of defeat. After a minute's walk I called out a spontaneous "Yay!" I was on the right track after all.

Once on the train, I started thinking about Ned, and how I'd been somewhat appalled on our first date to learn that he was a gambler. I thought back to a Saturday evening, years ago, when the five of us, children and my parents, were eating dinner. Papa had been arguing with my mother in Arabic.

"Yes, I am certainly going to tell them," he'd said in English, pounding the table. My mother shrugged and helplessly raised her arms.

"I'm going to tell all you children a true story," he began. "To teach you how a fine, upright man can fall from a high mountain"— he raised his arm—"from as high as the sky to the below gutter." We listened, wide-eyed, glad it wasn't one of us who had incurred his wrath.

"This happened a few days ago," he said. "Mr. Aboulafia, a man I do business with, lost his entire fortune, every penny he possessed, and some that were not his, at a French casino. He was playing roulette. Gambling. He entered the casino rich and highly respected and left poor and dishonored."

We didn't remember him, nor did we realize how much he'd lost, since a shilling piece to us was a fortune. Still, knowing he'd lost all his money evoked our sympathy.

Sensing this, my father bellowed, red-faced. "Children! You donkeys! A man who risks sending his wife and children to the poorhouse to satisfy his own greed is"—he spat out the word— "scum." The word was like a whip. We looked at one other, not daring to laugh.

That night I asked Sally, in the bed next to mine, what "scum" meant.

"Well, it's like that gray bubbly mush you see sometimes in the washbasin." Then she added, sleepily, "It's disgusting and it clings to the basin."

Disappointed, I asked, "Are you sure? That's all it means?"

She didn't deign to reply. I lay in the dark, wondering why my father thought the man who'd lost his fortune resembled gray bubbles. Maybe in the Arabic tirade he had shouted worse insults at Mr. Aboulafia.

For several weeks afterward, "scum" was our favorite word. It held a certain power in spite of its odd meaning. We loved it in all its variations. "You ate my chocolate, you scum!" or " Max did a scummy thing to me," or in a board game, "A scummish move, you've made."

Leaving the metro now and walking the short distance to the train station, my thoughts turned back to Ned. Paris should have been filled with gray fog or rain, as it often was in November. It would be less of an ache for Ned to be leaving. Instead, the sun sailed in and out of the clouds in the bluest of skies, bathing the roofs and streets in a shimmer of pale light.

My first look at the Gard du Nord made me stop. Built in the neoclassical style, with huge rounded windows and broad pillars, the building was unexpectedly pleasing. For a few moments the spidery rays of the sun turned it into a golden palace. A clock on high told me I was ten minutes early, after all.

Inside the station it was all crowds, noise, and bustle. But it wasn't hard to find the platform where the train for Le Havre stood waiting. Everywhere porters in blue moved up and down, pushing carts laden with trunks, suitcases, and hatboxes, shouting "*Attention!*"

Alongside the train, looking for compartment 54C, I made my way through throngs of people. Many passengers had already boarded. Conversations in a half-dozen tongues were flying about, and it seemed that just about everybody held a lighted cigarette. I hurried past couples tearfully embracing and mothers holding up babies to be kissed, and I nearly tripped on an old man who'd decided to take a step backwards and wound up treading on my toe. But where in heaven was 54C? My stomach lurched. Was I on the wrong platform?

Peering down to the far end of the train, I saw a flaxen mop moving. Could it be him? It was. Ned was leaning out the window. When I reached him, we just looked at each other, smiling broadly for several seconds.

And suddenly he was on the platform, his arms around me, kissing my cheeks and eyes. Then his mouth was on mine, his fingers in my hair. We forgot the station and the train standing beside us. A current of warmth rose up my body. When we separated we were breathing heavily, close and happy.

"Moments like that I'll take with me for whenever I'm lonely for you," he said. "And for Paris."

I felt my eyes starting to prickle.

"Lord, Glynne! Before I forget, I have something for you." He reached into a burlap bag on his shoulder and handed me two beautifully wrapped packages. "The one with the red ribbon is yours, the pink is Cathy's."

"Oh, Ned, you shouldn't have," I said earnestly. "Where did you find the time? With all you had to do, why did you even dream of shopping?"

He shrugged, pleased. "How could I not?"

"But you've given me books and records galore. I've given you bloody nothing, except that antique tie pin from the *Marchée aux Puces*. And," I said, giggling, "you may even have paid for it."

He covered my mouth with his hand. "Darling! I make a lot more money than you do. So please don't get quid pro quo on me. Remember, presents are fun for the giver, not an obligation for the receiver."

I liked the way that Ned dropped a Latin phrase into the sentence. "I don't like tit for tat either," I said, "but—"

"Stop. Don't rob me of the kick I get from giving you small nothings."

"Okay," I said. "And will you give me a hint of what's inside these gorgeously wrapped parcels? I can't open them here."

"Whoops!" he replied. Dammit! Hold on . . .I've got to get back on the train for a sec." He slung his bag firmly on his shoulder. "I left a suitcase—unlocked—with some pretty big bills in the overhead rack. I am 'daft" as you'd say." He punched his head lightly. "After I closed my account with Credit Lyonnais, I changed all my francs into dollars—lots of bucks—then shoved the wads of money into that case. It's probably okay ... likely still on the rack ... Better make sure." He headed for the steps, turning back to say, "When I left the compartment, there were just two women, but by now any oddball could be in there." He glanced at his watch. "We've got more than twenty minutes before the train leaves."

At that moment, a stout man in a navy blue uniform blew a whistle and began speaking through a megaphone in French then in English. "All passengers must board the train IMMEDIATELY."

So in two minutes, we were back to our earlier position, me on the platform and Ned in the corridor outside his compartment, which held six people comfortably, three on each side facing one another with plenty of leg room. He gave me a thumbs up sign. "It's right up there. Guess what? Two new passengers occupy my compartment. Englishmen, I think; five now, all told." His eyes gleamed. "More than enough for a rubber of bridge, wouldn't you say?"

I shook my head. He was incorrigible. An expert player. A gambler.

"Low stakes . . . natch, " he added, and lighting a cigarette, he inhaled deeply. "Okay. For Cathy I found a maternal-looking mouse. Her eyes are somewhat bizarre—they swivel like this." He demonstrated, rolling his eyeballs in circles. "When she sees the big floppy *chapeau* and checked apron, she'll know exactly who it is. How about you?"

"*Naturellement!*" I said, laughing. "It's the wise *Madame Souris*. Cathy will hit the ceiling with joy."

"As for you, I got you records, not for a change. One is the new long-play album of Yves Montand. I listened to part of it. Wow! It's something. I was bowled over. When you write, tell me the songs you like the most."

"Oh Ned," I wailed, "it won't be the same not listening to them together."

"C'mon, darling. We'll get through this separation one way or the other." After a pause, he said, "You know, what really galls me is why the devil in the nearly five months we've known each other we've never slept together. Why was that. do you suppose?"

"Well, even when a fellow appeals to me, I don't leap into bed with him," I explained. "For the first three months we were getting to know each other. And when we were getting closer, that bad Théo thing happened. Remember how much we were both looking forward to the Yves Montand concert?"

"My gala dinner," he said. "Not too gala afterward. Glynne, I can't tell you how much I'm going to miss you. Lucky you to be in Paris. You'll make other friends. It's your nature. But I want us to be friends for life. So don't ever give me the brush-off."

"What a beastly thing to say, Ned! Say you're sorry."

He lowered his chin humbly. "Christ, I guess I'm halfway in love with you. I'm already jealous of the guys you'll be seeing in Paris." He stopped and bit his lip. "You know, it's incredible, but I don't have any pictures of you. I'd give anything for just one nice photo to remind me of how you look."

"I don't have any of you, either. Send me one, too."

He nodded and turned his head. "Hey, I'll be back in a jiffy." He retreated to the inside of the car.

In that moment, I knew exactly what to do, what I could give him. I took out my green-backed passport, then my Swiss Army knife with its neat little scissors. In less than a minute, I'd cut out the picture from my passport. I studied it. As an identity photo it wasn't at all bad. When he came back to the window, I was excited.

"Here, Ned. I've got something for you."

He reached down and took the photo, then saw the passport still in my hand. He gasped. "Glynne, you haven't—I mean, what the hell have you done?"

"I have, and the picture's for you. It was taken more than a year ago, but it's the only one I've got. I think it's quite nice, really."

His jaw was open. He snapped it closed and said, "I can't quite believe what you did."

"Oh, don't go on Ned. You'll spoil the present. It's only a picture, after all. I can easily replace it with another. I can explain my way out of it if they fuss."

Before he could reply I told him what my sister Sally had said to me when I had lost my matriculation certificate. "Always remember that whatever stupid thing you do, you won't be the first. Someone has done it already."

Ned looked at me glassy-eyed. Then all at once his eyes were twinkling. "Darling, darling Glynne, in this instance, your sister could be wrong. You may just be the very first . . . " Ned was smiling, shaking his head. When the whistle blew for the last time, we were both convulsed with laughter.

The train started to move. My jaw was aching from laughing. I watched Ned hanging out the window waving, laughing still, then kissing my picture, until he disappeared from view.

Chapter Thirty-one

I left the Gard du Nord still seeing Ned's laughing face. I'd always liked the way he laughed. His body seemed to cave forward independently, as though released by a spring.

Reaching la rue de Dunkerque, I sat on a bench, my book bag and his good-bye presents next to me, my eyes misty. I scolded myself much the way Miss Verity, my physics teacher, had when I was in the fifth form. I hadn't thought about her for years. "Glynne, you must break your habit of wandering off in the clouds if you expect to be a physicist." Walking home with my best chum, Sylvia, we got to imitating that dear woman. Sylvia had wagged a finger at me and announced in Miss Verity's classy voice, "My dear girl. An opening has suddenly come up for a director on North England's Board of Physics. Possibly a position for you, except they do *not* want"—Sylvia's voice rose sternly—"fabricators or daydreamers."

I looked at my watch. Heavens! How memories ensnare one. I pulled out my *Plan de Paris par arrondissement*, a small brown hardback. This book, a feat of precision, was carried by almost every Parisian. It showed every street in Paris's twenty *arrondissements* and the nearest metro station. It provided the addresses of theatres, museums, monuments, churches, embassies, even swimming pools.

I discovered that the American Embassy was on the avenue Gabriel, at the northwest corner of the place de la Concorde. The metro would get me there in fifteen minutes.

Once my new photo had been taken, developed, and inserted into that gaping hole on page three of my passport, I'd return to the Left Bank, lighthearted and free. I'd even have time for lunch at Geneviève, my cafeteria, where I'd probably bump into people

I knew, before taking off for my phonetics class with M. Poivrot, my favorite teacher. He'd begun our last class by saying, "Do you realize how important lips are?" The class had tittered. "*Eh bien!* They need to be strong if zey are French lips." More laughter. "I refer only to making sounds," he'd said. He'd shown us how to push out our mouths forcefully for that characteristic French "oo" sound—"*nounou*" (nanny), "*nouvelles*" (news)—and we all had to shout "*Oh là là, oh là là*" whenever he paused.

We'd watch his mouth, trying to arrange ours like his for words like *tulipier* (tulip tree), *fructeusement* (fruitfully), and *conglutinant* (sticky). "Not everyday words," he'd admitted. "But, *messieurs et mademoiselles*, zis is an exercise. Make sure each syllable is pronounced correctly, then"—he'd made a gesture as though winding up a toy—"increase your speed until you say the whole word. Say it fast. Even faster. When that 'appens"—he snapped his fingers—"then you 'ave confidence. You 'ave fluidity. You are speaking French."

I closed my eyes and lay back against the wood planks, breathing in the cool air, the November sun glancing over my eyelids and cheeks. How often had I sat with Ned sipping coffee on a day like this! I was going to miss him. I was lonely for him already. Dear, dear Ned! Would I ever have fallen for him totally? Probably not. But I'd taken for granted we'd go on and on having fun. His leaving Paris jettisoned a galaxy of possibilities.

Light footsteps nearby made me jump. I straightened up and saw opposite me a slip of a boy, thirteen or fourteen, staring at me. His jacket was far too big and his curly hair matted. I noticed he was holding onto a cigarette butt. He approached me nonchalantly, his eyes, dark blue with curly black lashes, unsmiling. "*Avez-vous du feu?*" Do you have a light? He inserted the stub between his lips.

"I don't smoke," I said.

"*Pas de blague?*" Are you kidding? It was almost a reprimand.

He removed the butt, inserting it carefully in his pocket. He was defiant yet somehow vulnerable.

"Wait!" I riffled through my purse and produced an opened pack of gum. "How about chewing gum? Would you a like a piece?"

He scowled. "Okay."

There were five sticks left. He took three from the pack.. Ramming two in his pocket, he tossed the last one up in the air and caught it neatly in his mouth. *"Merci"* he nodded at me and started to chew vigorously.

"Attention Attention! Ne l'avale pas!" I warned, *"On peut s'étouffer."* Be careful. Don't swallow it. You could choke. Few Parisians chewed gum. He walked alongside my bench. Then abruptly halted. He'd stopped chewing. Both hands were clutched around his throat and he gasped as if he were strangling. His face had become contorted. I rose to my feet. What was going on?

He leaped into the air with a shriek. Back on his feet he whirled around once, then slowly started to saunter by me with his chin high. Pleased by his act, he gave me a devilish grin.

Chapter Thirty-two

Emerging from the metro, I took in the spaciousness of the place de la Concorde and the obelisk of yellow granite rising in its center. The obelisk's appeal was more than that of an exquisite artifact; it had stood in the land of Egypt for over three thousand years before it was given as a gift to France in 1883.

I had no trouble finding the American embassy, with its American flag fluttering over the four-story building nearby. I touched a small button and heard a gong resonate. A plump man in a uniform with gold trim stood in front of me.

"Bonjour, *Mademoiselle*." He smiled in a pleasant way, correctly.

"Hello," I said, speaking in English, thinking he'd follow suit.

"*Eh bien*, what can I do for you?" he replied in French

"I'd like to speak to someone about my passport, please."

"*Non, non*—no speak Eenglish." He vigorously waved a forefinger in front of his nose. After a moment, he asked "Passport?" It is the same word in both languages. He watched as I wrote my name on his pad, then led me to a room wallpapered in a repeat pattern of men fencing.

"You're lucky, we're not very busy," he said. "You'll be speaking to Mr. Gilmore. Make yourself comfortable." He smiled, handed me an English newspaper, and left.

I sat on one of the hard cushions and began planning what to say. Knowing nothing about Mr. Gilmore, I needed to have a strategy. Scenario one would be if he seemed strict and solemn. The key here was not to be too twinkly or brimming with fun. The path to a steely heart surely would be paved with mortification and anxiety. I'd fill any silences with heartfelt apologies, which by this time might very well be genuine.

Scenario two was better. In this one, Gilmore was understanding, a man with a touch of humor. I'd explain why I'd acted rashly at the train station with Ned, emphasizing Ned's good nature; how he'd packed everything up in two days to reach his mother who'd fractured her hip; and finally, how sad he'd seemed not having even one photo to remember me by. I could see a half-smile curving Mr. Gilmore's lips and hear his paternal words: "It's all right, my dear. We all make mistakes. It's nothing to worry about. I will take care of the matter." I'd tell him how terribly grateful I was, and this would be true.

Scenario three was my favorite. "Now what's this all about?" Gilmore would ask in a hearty, avuncular manner. He'd peer into the gaping hole in my passport, then, throwing his head back, would burst out laughing. After which he'd beam at me, his face pink with mirth, and say something like, "Well, you have been a naughty girl, haven't you? From now on, no snipping pictures out of passports, eh? Scout's honor?" And he'd take my hand in his while I repeated, my eyes dancing, "Girl Guide's honor," and off he'd lumber to make me a new photo.

I needed more work on scenario one, Gilmore-the-strict. Better to start with something like, "Mr. Gilmore, you're probably going to think that what I've done is immature, even reprehensible." I'd apologize for my temporary insanity, which I'd explain took place a minute before the train moved. But I hadn't *torn* out the passport picture: I'd *cut* it out neatly with scissors. Then I'd play my ace: how the pain of Ned's imminent absence . . . I never finished my thought. A shiver slid down my spine. Suppose he noticed from my passport that I was a Mrs.? Then he'd surmise that my passion was for a man other than my husband. As a faithless wife, everything would go against me. He might even think I was posing as a student. The tangle of possible difficulties took my breath away.

Abruptly, an inner door opened. A middle-aged woman in a brown dress called out my name and led me into a large airy room. At the far end, a tall man in a dark jacket sat at a desk facing an enormous window, his back to me. Another, youngish fellow in a gray suit could be seen in a glass alcove, leafing through a pile of papers. He looked up at me for a few seconds, returning my smile with a prim one of his own. I followed the woman in brown noiselessly on my crepe soles until she stopped at the big desk, where she placed a folder and announced my name in a scratchy voice. "Will that be all, sir?"

A clear voice answered. "Would you make time, please, to work on the red reference file?" It didn't sound like a question

She said quickly, "Yes, sir," and padded off.

After I'd been standing for a short while, Mr. Gilmore's hand flipped up above the back of his chair, forefinger gesturing in the air toward the right. I assumed he meant the chair, and I sat down. Another pause. I coughed gently and he wheeled around stiffly, still seated, to face me. "Good afternoon, Mrs. Nahem." His eyes were the color of light jade.

"I've come about my passport," I blurted, my scenarios all forgotten. "You see, I need to get a new picture."

"Yes?" He had a long face and a full head of brownish-gray hair. He threw me a quizzical look. "Not happy with the old one?"

His bemused question so lightly asked set off a quiet explosion in my head. My heart skipped. He'd pointed the way to a new scenario, one I hadn't considered. Rather than be condemned as a no-good hussy who was two-timing her husband, I could choose to be a self-centered narcissist who couldn't bear people looking at a bad picture of her. I had been ashamed of it!

"Well, it was quite hideous. I don't have it anymore. The thing is—"

He threw out a long arm. "Show me the passport, please."

He opened it briskly and saw the big gaping hole where my picture had been. And in a second he was on his feet, a lamppost of a man, towering over me. The pale eyes bored into mine. "Precisely who caused this mutilation?"

"I did."

"You!" He recoiled. "You dared to desecrate an emblem of the United States of America?" The trembling in his voice betrayed his rage. He didn't seem to expect an answer. To avoid being paralyzed by his fury, I kept my gaze on the high ceiling. I braved a glance at him, noticed his flushed cheeks and mottled neck, and was glad I had kept silent.

He sat back down. "Is there anything you can say in your defense?" His expression was grim. He began tapping on the desk with his pencil, and I knew I'd never reveal the truth about Ned kissing and waving the passport photo from the window as the train disappeared. Mr. Gilmore would have apoplexy .

"Nobody ever recognized me in that picture," I said. "There was no resemblance. Not the faintest. I should never have used it for such an important document." Carried away by my new role in the drama, I elaborated. "When I registered at the Sorbonne I was given a hard time. The man kept saying, 'This cannot possibly be you,' and he made me step aside, and there was a terrible fuss." I shook my head. "It really was a hideous photo."

"I see you are endowed with an abundance both of vanity and conceit. That is a problem I can do little about. However," he said coolly, "perhaps two or three weeks in prison might curb your rash tendencies with scissors. Possibly I might send you back home to New York immediately, and your passport would be rescinded."

My legs turned to jelly. Was he kidding? Not likely, with that steely voice. I could think of nothing to say in my defense.

Instead, what came out of me was a mangled moan. "Please, oh please, do neither of those things. I really am sorry." I desperately didn't want to go to jail or return to New York. Before I had entered his office it had all seemed a bit of a joke. Now the larkiness was gone, and my scenarios along with it. How could just one misguided action beget such scary consequences?

"Mr. Gilmore," I said, "When I cut out my picture it was not to dishonor the United States. It was just a thoughtless, irresponsible act of the moment. I wish I hadn't done it."

"You weren't born in the U.S., I gather from your accent."

"I have dual citizenship, English and American."

"I see. Clearly, what you don't recognize, Mrs. Nahem, is that a United States passport is a privilege. It alone enables you to leave the United States, enter another country, stay in it for a period of time, and return by a specific date. It also entitles you to protection of several kinds. As an important example, you might be in a country which becomes threatening but allows you no exit. Then you can take shelter within the American Embassy, where you will be safe and inviolable. Possibly you are unaware that American passports are valuable the world over. There are people who steal them from innocent citizens, make a few alterations, and sell them for several thousand dollars to criminals."

I shook my head. "I didn't know that." I was swayed by the breadth of his eloquence and information.

"I'm a believer in punishment," he said.

My heart sank.

"It clarifies things for the wrongdoer."

I knew I was in for it.

"This time I am not going to have you locked up, nor will you be sent back to New York. I sense you have learned something today. Correct me if I'm wrong."

I bit my lips and kept back the tears. Relief sank through me. Even while shivering, I answered, "What you just said, I simply hadn't thought of it that way."

"I am imposing a penalty that you can easily endure." He looked at me coldly. "One you may possibly remember all your life. You are to appear here each day for the next two weeks starting tomorrow. On your arrival, you will sit at that table"—he pointed—"where you'll find sheets of lined paper with a different first line each day, selected by myself. Tomorrow, Tuesday, the line will be "I pledge allegiance to the flag of the United States of America." You will copy this sentence three hundred times, after which you may leave."

I thanked him for my punishment.

At last, he half-smiled, and I saw that his long face was quite handsome.

"When you've completed the two weeks, I'll return your passport to you," he continued. "The gentleman here will take your snapshot. However," he added, a faint amusement in his eyes, "I cannot vouch for its being everything you expect in a picture."

"I deserve a horrid one," I said firmly. After thanking him, I found myself saying, unbelievably, "I look forward to seeing you tomorrow."

That evening I called David at the *Daily Mail* and told him what had happened. He repeated slowly, "Wait, Glynne. You cut out your passport photo?" He sounded baffled. "I think you need looking after, chum. What got into your head?"

"David, no lecture, please. I've just had one. Tell me: could Mr. Gilmore really have me locked up, or was he just trying to scare me?"

"I think he could," David said. "All said, ducks, you seem to have got off pretty lightly."

Chapter Thirty-three

Three weeks after Ned left I received his first letter.

"Glynne darling,

"*Bonjour!* So how's Paris without me? Likely you're thinking 'He's gone, yet Paris is still Paris. It can never lose its glow.' And you'd be right—sometimes you are!

"Surprise, Glynne, guess what? I'm sort of glad to be back here, for a spell, at least. I am drunk often in the usual way, but now I am drunk from gaping at all the space here. You just can't believe how the land really merges with the sky, and sunsets and dawns have more colors than a paint box. High up driving my tractor, wind in my ears, with the scents of earth and corn and grass in my nostrils . . . it's kinda my song, well for now—a million miles from Paris.

"How's Cathy? Tell her I think about her, and don't let on I'm making her a wood cradle for Madame Mouse.

"Glynne, my *jolie chérie*, we really did have fun—well, even more than that, didn't we? I suppose it had to end. Did it? I knew from the start you weren't sure of your feelings toward me. So I've had to let go of mine. One thing, it goes without saying, you and me, we'll be friends forever. *Je t'embrasse très fort.*

"Glynne, baby, you'll be okay. Thinking of you, Ned."

His letter left me with deeply contrary emotions. I was surprised at how much it captured his voice and left me near tears. And while I felt slightly miffed that he wasn't pining for me, I also felt relief that it was over. Our fling or adventure or whatever it had been was not love for me and had reached an end. Now we could both get on with our lives.

Overall, I felt buoyed up somehow by this and his next letter in a similar vein. I responded: "Thank you, dear Ned, for the appealing picture of Indiana and lack of maudlin sentiments. Happy, too, that you're glad be home in Indiana and for the good news about your mother." I told him about Cathy's first acting role, as a tree in her school play. And how Madame Tourdzie made us write an eight-line poem in French.

"I'll always treasure our times together and all the talks we had. We had such fun, especially because we didn't always see eye-to-eye. It made it more than ordinary fun. So I'd like to have a photo of you. I'll show it to Cathy when she says 'I just want to see Ned.' Any picture will do, not necessarily one snipped from your passport!"

I also wrote how being with him in Paris had added a glow to it all and that knowing we'd stay friends forever was wonderful and made the world seem smaller.

I ended, "Ned, you're terribly missed. You can guess. But your mother must be glad to have you back. I dearly hope she'll be striding about soon—don't leave ladders anywhere nearby. With like and love. A bit of both. *Avec grande affection,* Glynne."

Actually, I missed him acutely at first. The absence of a dear companion, one who is fun, handsome, and easy to be with, is a lonely business. But at least the tussle with my conscience about going all the way with a lovely guy I did not love all the way was settled.

Cathy, while she still missed Ned, became more involved with her schoolmates. She'd become close with three girls in her class, and her sentences often began importantly, "When Marie, Chantal, Vinca, and I" were painting or rolling the hoop or playing ball or singing"—here she'd glance at me to check that I was impressed before finishing her sentence.

She admitted, "Marie, Chantal, and Vinca always did things together, but now it's me with them." She told me proudly how the class had to make a poster so that people would come to the school play. "And Mlle Brissard pointed at us and said, 'What is our little *quatuor* going to do?' What a funny word. *Maman,* try to guess what it means."

I held up four fingers.

She squealed, "*Maman!* How did you know?"

"What is four in French?"

She tapped her head and said, "*Bien sûr, je comprends*"—"Of course, I understand."

My classes at the Sorbonne now ended at two o clock. I didn't pick up my daughter from her play group until five. With Ned gone, this gift of time, three hours, stretched out invitingly but not without anxiety. What would I do with it? I vowed not to let it slip away shopping, cooking, and darning socks. I began reading in the afternoons. I was a few chapters into the first volume of the ten-volume, *Jean-Christophe* by Romain Rolland. My bookseller on the *quai* was aghast I'd never even heard of it. He hadn't minced words. "You cannot consider yourself educated unless you've read it. *C'est du tonnerre*"—"It's fantastic."

I staggered off, the big book in my arms. He called after me, "Eh, *mademoiselle*, Romain Rolland taught music for years at the Sorbonne. "

Some people called me *mademoiselle*, some called me *madame*.

Curled up on Mme Doucet's old couch, my legs under a rug, a French dictionary at hand, I studied the tattered dust jacket. "It is the most original, boldest, and healthiest work of the 20th century." Healthiest? How droll. Did it cleanse the mind? Unlikely. I also learned that Romain Rolland had won the Nobel prize for this book in 1915.

Having nearly forgotten the exquisite joy of reading for pleasure rather than for school, I was delighted to live in a different country, an earlier century with bizarre rules of propriety, where strong-minded middle-class women wore taffetas and silks. After gobbling up about a quarter of the book, I found the manly Jean-Christophe, based on Beethoven, almost perfect. Who wouldn't settle for a guy who could hum glorious melodies at breakfast, who hated war, who could be gentle yet strong, and whose looks were equal to Jean Gabin's?

When Jean-Christophe becomes stone deaf, I was devastated. I was living this book so intensely that when I laid it down I was often startled to see I was in my own living room with its little coal stove.

I knew I needed to do other things besides reading. Still, my axiom "when enjoying yourself, do more of it" held up. When my bookseller told me about André Gide, I watched how his eyes glittered when he said that Catholicism had been Gide's inspiration as well as his silencer. I tried to make sense of the paradox and it made me late for class. *Tant pis!*—So what? *Carpe diem!*

So when Cathy and I were passing an iron-railing fence and she begged me to stop so she could squeeze her toes between the rails and walk this odd way to the end, I let her. She took a long time and we were late for her school again. But in her fashion, I thought, she had seized the day.

I thought back to how Joe, from the start, had taken charge of most of our lives: which events to go to, which friends to have for dinner, how to get to the cinema on time, and how to budget our funds. Organizing for him was like breathing. In Paris, after our *petit déjeuner*, he'd pull out a notebook and announce plans for us. "The best film ever made, *Potemkin*, with French subtitles, is around the corner. We could eat at home or in a restaurant. Anywhere's fine except La Cotelette, where the pork chop took out my filling." Later it was Ned who procured tickets for the concerts and plays and took me to the occasional restaurant.

But now I was starting a new era. My vague plan was to allow for more spontaneity, to explore different parts of Paris, and to renew bonds with old friends. I vowed to be more organized and practical.

I bought a leather diary, light, thin, and expensive, to be used for dates, places, times, and notes. In the shop, I hadn't noticed that three full days were squashed onto a single page; I'd been too busy complimenting the owner on its soft leather. Just the name of a Hungarian restaurant took up a full page. I wrote in smaller letters, later unreadable, so I hardly mourned when I lost the leather diary.

I started to go for walks with Tamara, David's wife. I'd always wanted to know her better. Now five months pregnant, she'd be waiting for me on a bench facing the Seine. From a small way off, sitting dreamily with her ankles crossed, she reminded me of Vishnu, a Hindu deity. In my brother's room I'd often seen Vishnu's picture, the face filled with the same benign contentment. I'd asked Eddy why her bosom was so low-slung. My big brother had tapped my head. "Idiot! Vishnu is a male." I'd studied the picture, trying unsuccessfully to change the she into a he.

Tamara and I always crowned our walks near the river with *un chocolat bien chaud*—a really hot chocolate. We'd order one croissant, virtuously breaking it in two. Then, creamy froth on our lips, relaxed by the exercise, we'd talk. Watching her brown eyes shining and cheeks glowing, I told her she'd become lovelier with pregnancy.

She frowned. "But my hips get bigger each day. I'm like a ripe pear." She leaned forward. "I'm scared they'll stay big even after the baby's born. It happened to my mother."

"But that was at a time when pregnant women were supposed to eat for two," I said. "Besides, yours haven't changed. Anyway, men really go for hips and bosoms. They can't get enough of them. You'll be the rage."

She nibbled on her croissant. "I just couldn't bear it if David stopped loving me."

"*Jamais!* That man is insane for you. The more of you there is, the happier he'll be. I've known David longer than you have. He's not a flirt."

"It's true, he doesn't eye other women. But you never know what gorgeous blonde he'll meet at the office."

After we had drained our cups to the last dregs, I told her about what Leon had told me long ago, that I would never fall in love. He had even invoked his belated mother.

"What a creep to involve his dead mother!" Tamara responded. She probably turned in her grave at the lie. But what do you care about what that moron said?"

"Well, it's true so far. I've never fallen in love."

"C'mon, silly," she kidded. "Proust said we all fall in love when we're ready and want to love someone. So start getting ready."

When she left, she kissed me twice on the left cheek and once on the right, for luck. Her last words were, "M. Proust knew what he was talking about."

Ned's absence was a catalyst that took Cathy and me to new directions. I started going to exhibitions at some of the lesser-known museums, sometimes with Hedrik from class. (I refrained from asking him if Mme Tourdzie's French "sexy love words" had done the trick with his wife, Marieka.) Or I'd meet Marieka at M. Roland's record shop.

One time I went back with her to their tiny apartment. In the bathroom there was a strange, shiny helmet with a long tube coming out of it. I held it aloft. "Are you taking up deep-sea diving? What is this weird contraption?"

"It's called a Massosein. It's to stop your breasts from sagging. You attach the tube to the cold water faucet, arrange one of your breasts in the helmet, then turn on the water and *whee!* Cold water flies around it in circles."

She explained that it had actually been a man who had demonstrated it in the street. A woman in the crowd had shouted, "Yours are so flat, there's nothing to sag." He'd sold quite a few to older women. "He seemed quite surprised when I bought one."

"Me too." I said. "Yours are so uptilted and small. You could fit the two of them together into that thing."

"Mine aren't bad, I admit," she said. "But anyway, the water swishing around"—she made a circular gesture with her hand—"makes your nipples stick out afterward. Very sexy."

"For how long?"

"Everyone's different. Mine stay for nearly an hour." She paused. "They say when you have a baby, breasts change for the bigger."

I opened my eyes wide. Mareika said hastily, "Nothing's on the way yet, but Hedrik is hoping." She held out the Massosein. "Want to try it?"

"Sometime, yes, but I'm not sure I'd fit. It's not that I'm saggy, but I'm undeniably big. Sometimes I envy your rosebuds."

"And I envy yours! I'd like Hedrik to have a nice handful."

I left the apartment thoughtfully, my education having taken a new turn. And Marieka, whom I thought of as beautiful, wasn't quite so timid as I'd thought. I wondered perhaps if it hadn't been her idea for Hedrik to ask Mme Tourdzie about exciting love talk in French.

At this time, without any prodding, Cathy had again become interested in her wind-up record player (*tourne-disques*), and for the first time in months she listened to her French nursery rhymes. She warbled along with the singer and pranced about. If I were nearby she'd call out, "*Maman*, quick, it's your favorite, '*J'ai perdu le do de ma clarinette.*'" Then, clutching imaginary clarinets, we would bellow out the words loud enough to bring the walls tumbling down. Or I'd see her on the floor with her special colored blocks that had archways and walls. She'd call something like, "I've made three different castles. Let's knock them down together."

She was branching out in other ways, too. She told me a secret that worried her. She sat up in her blue flannel nightgown and spoke in a tremulous voice. "My friends told me . . . something. They said Éric and Jean, who I don't like, told Béatrice they'd give her some money if they could see her . . . " She paused. "Her derriere. I said, 'Éric wouldn't do that.' They said Éric is not bad, but Jean kept after him to ask Béatrice."

It wasn't a pretty story. I decided to confront Éric, whom I knew, and quietly talk to him, saying he'd done something wrong and disrespectful to another person. If he promised never to repeat it, I wouldn't go to Mlle Brissard. I might even talk to Béatrice. Cathy seemed calmer after telling me, and I said firmly, "Don't worry, things will be all right from now on."

The next day, I spoke to Éric. He was petrified and began to cry. "I never wanted to. It was Jean. I didn't even want even to look. I hope Jesus will forgive me!"

Jean was stronger and taller than most of his classmates. He listened to me, his head in the air. He was sullen until I said, "You can be expelled for this, did you know?" He didn't answer. He began to rub his eyes. "Please, Miss, don't tell my father. He'll whip me." Soon he was crying and imploring me not to report him. "Don't tell my *papa*! I'll never do it again, I promise!"

There were daily rehearsals for the school play, *Little Red Riding Hood*. Paul, still Cathy's favorite, was the wolf. "He's so savage, he scares me," she said. "You'll see."

At first she'd been sad not to be chosen as Red Riding Hood, but now she was happy, putting her heart into her role as a tree. It moaned and waved from side to side in the wind. At a meeting of the children and their parents, she asked wistfully if the tree might have a small voice. Everyone laughed. Mlle. Brissard turned to her and said, "Yes. You can create a tree language, little noises in the wind. Make sure they're low."

The first days after Ned had left, Cathy had asked, "*Maman*, is he going to live on his farm for always?" Now her question was more philosophical: "Can you stay friends with somebody you never see?"

"What do you think?" I said, dodging a complicated answer.

She frowned. "Well, suppose I didn't see Ned until I was ten or twelve. He'd go on thinking of me as being five."

"He'd picture you as five, perhaps, but he'd know that picture wasn't how you looked now. Every New Year would remind him you'd grown older. And if you wanted, you could send him a photo each year so he could see you change."

"But photos can't see your mind," she persisted, "and he wouldn't know the thoughts inside me."

"Well, Cathy," I said lamely, "you'd still be friends. You'd write letters that told him what you were doing and thinking."

Chapter Thirty-four

Two days later, on a brisk fall day, I went as usual to my student cafeteria, Geneviève, and found that most of the tables were filled. My new outgoing outlook took me and my tray to a table occupied by two fellows and a girl, with one empty place. Their chatter stopped as they smiled a welcome at me. As was the custom, the fellows rose, waiting until I was seated. One had gray eyes in a dimpled face; the other was dark-haired and handsome.

I told them my name, and the gray-eyed one made the introductions. He was Eugène. The girl, who had pouty lips and short coif, was Sylvie, and the dark-haired fellow was Patrice.

Eugène said amicably, "*J'ai l'idée que vous n'êtes pas française?*"—"I assume you're not French?" He'd used *vous* as a sign of respect, rather than the more familiar *tu*.

Patrice glanced at my tray. "Whatever her nationality, Glynne is classy. Why else would she be treated to a pork chop, apple stew, and brown rice, while the rest of us got chopped meat and spuds?"

With delighted grins, they thumped their fists on the table and cried, "*À nous les cotelettes!*"—"Chops for all!"

Sylvie explained, "We're students at the Beaux Arts and usually eat at our own cafeteria. Today we lost track of time in the bookstores on the Boul'Mich, and so—"

Eugene gracefully finished her sentence, "so we decided to meet you here, instead."

Before I could open my mouth, Patrice said, "But admit it, aren't you a just little bit glad you came to our table?"

"Honored," I said, "and surprised. I thought students had to dine at the *foyer* assigned to them."

"No, you can dine at any *foyer* so long as you carry a student card." Eugène raised his arms in the national gesture of "that's the way it is." "I didn't know that at the beginning, either," he said. "In my first year at Beaux Arts I dined with a friend from the École des Mines, and I thought they might expel me for it."

"You? The star student? Nevaire," Sylvie said in a mock English. She flung her elbow around his neck.

Sylvie told me that everybody called Eugène, who was her boyfriend, Gene, short for *génie*—genius—"which he actually is. He's top boy at Beaux Arts," she added, snuggling close to him.

"Sylvie, darling, don't bore Glynne so soon," he said.

I was hugely enjoying myself. I admired their elegance, their style, their intelligence, and, most of all, their streak of rationality.

Patrice proposed that we all lunch at Geneviève the same day next week.

Then Sylvie turned to me. "We'll all be graduating in three months. God, I can't bear the thought. I'll miss my friends, the teachers—everything."

"I'm going to miss the ancient buildings, the rotten wood staircases, and the tunnels for corridors," Eugène said. "Not to mention the never-ending small rooms."

I said I loved those buildings from the outside but had never been in them.

Eugène immediately offered me a tour. "Be outside the main building at three-thirty on Friday."

"I'll be there."

Patrice caught my eye and said, "Don't go in alone if Eugene is late. You'll never find your way out."

Chapter Thirty-five

On Friday I waited in the courtyard of the École des Beaux Arts. It was ten to four and Eugène still hadn't shown up. The autumn wind was sharp. I felt chilled and let down.

I began walking back toward the gates on the rue Bonaparte when I saw Patrice running toward me. Before I could speak, he said, panting, "Eugène isn't well. He has a migraine. He wanted me to tell you he can't take you around the buildings. I can show you around maybe for five minutes, but I must get back to him."

I was about to say that I would not think of taking a tour now, when somebody pushed him from behind.

Patrice wheeled around and saw a short blond fellow grinning at him. "Guy, hello, this is Glynne."

Guy nodded at me, smiling, and Patrice said, "Guy's a friend in my design class." He turned to him, "Hey, are you busy now, Guy?"

"No more than usual. Why?"

Patrick spoke French so fast I couldn't fathom it, but Guy listened intently, nodding. Then he turned to me.

"If you like, Glynne," he said, "I'll take you to see the oldest building for a short while."

Patrice said , "Go with him, Glynne. Eugène is alone and may need something. I'll see you at lunch next Wednesday." He touched my shoulder and sped away.

Guy beckoned. He pointed to a building near the courtyard. "It was built a long, long time ago, in 1601, and it has had little restoration, as you can see."

Soon I was following him up and down staircases in the semi-darkness. Here there were no *minuteries,* the timed electric lights. The worn wooden banisters were silky-smooth under my hand.

He was a few steps ahead of me, plodding up and down a warren of corridors and staircases. He didn't talk but regularly looked back to check on me. Once I almost tripped over my shoelace and clumsily tied it on one of the small, dark platforms. I rushed up the stairs after him but could see neither him nor anyone else. I listened for the sound of his shoes. Nothing. I ran back down the same flight of stairs, then back up an adjacent one that landed me on a sort of bridge. I was suddenly overcome with panic. How long would it take for me to get out of this castle of stairs?

I opened a door and with some relief saw about twenty male students, about my age, sitting in groups on top of desks, with a few high up on the windowsills. The talking stopped as I entered. In seconds, a phalanx of three stood guarding the door. The others surrounded me.

"I'm lost I think," I said. "The person I was following seems to have suddenly evaporated. Would someone please show me the way out?"

I felt uneasy waiting for an answer. I'd never before been in a similar situation. One of them introduced himself as Jules. He was a tall, without much expression. "I will show you out, gladly."

I smiled too soon.

He continued, "However, there is a ritual that goes back for more than a half- century that insists that any female entering this room is obliged to take off all her clothing. Nobody will harm you. Nobody will even touch you." There was a chorus of "*Nous le jurons.*"—"We swear to it." Jules added, "The last woman remained here for eleven hours because she was stubborn. We brought her coffee and croissants, however."

"You've got to be joking," I said, smiling. "Really, it is so infantile. I'm late, so please escort me out." One or two of them looked somewhat abashed. Someone shouted, "Explain it to her, Jules."

He answered, "I have already," then addressed me. "We really won't let you out, you know, until you undress. But after you're nude for just a few seconds, you can dress and be escorted out."

He wasn't kidding. I sat down on one of the desk tops, pulling my skirt over my knees. I was wearing a tailored wool suit. "I'll cut a deal with you," I said in passable French. "How about I sing you an English song? Or if you like I'll do an Irish jig, a funny hopping dance, if you let me out."

They shook their heads no. One explained, maddeningly, "You see, it is a historical ritual."

I glanced at my watch. For once I'd given myself some spare time. It was four o'clock. I needed to pick up Cathy at five-thirty, after her play rehearsal.

I appealed to them. "Don't you find this tradition just a bit archaic and anti-woman?"

Jules shrugged. "Nobody minds because nobody is harmed."

"The very idea harms me!" My voice emerged small and shrill. "I won't remove even one bobby pin from my hair."

A fellow on the window ledge clapped, while others hissed and stuck their thumbs downward.

"As you wish, *Mademoiselle,*" said Jules.

I saw a wide-eyed student in a corner sitting on his haunches. My eyes met his, and I stopped because he was speaking gently to me, with a touch of worry in his voice. He spoke in broken English and with sincerity. "Zey really will not 'arm you." He shook his head. "We all respect ze old traditions in France." He had a sensitive face, and his eyes made me think of an eagle's.

I was about to make another speech when the door opened. A professor with a long gray beard slowly walked in. The students, as one, sprang back to their desks, and I, lithe as a cat, sprang out the door.

Even though I stepped down staircases that led nowhere, I was careful to open no more doors, and after several mistakes I found my way out. I breathed in the cold air. I wanted to laugh and cry at the same time. Freedom is ecstasy after you've been robbed of it, even for a short time. As I walked out through the high iron gates, I shouted, "Dammit to hell with your bloody infantile traditions and your piggy anti-woman lust."

I swept around the corner to the rue Bonaparte, furiously castigating the enemy. "You rotten swine, all of you. But you didn't get to see me in the altogether, did you?" I was overcome with crazy laughter. My fist raised high, I yelled into the air, "See! You lost and I won!" Passing a shop window, I saw a lunatic stamping her feet, one arm brandished high as though in battle.

Minutes later, I was sitting in a café nearby, comforting myself with a *café crème*, when a shadow moved across the table. I looked up and saw the fellow with the sympathetic face who'd spoken to me.

"Is it okay for me to sit?" he asked.

I nodded.

He half-smiled. "Are you okay?"

"I'm fine. I'm tougher than I look."

He asked me my name and I told him.

"Gleene" he repeated. "Like a church bell, *gleeng-gleeng.* I'm Maurice," he said.

He leaned forward. "Don't feel sad, not even a bit, at what 'appened. It's not so important."

"Would they really have kept me there for hours or days?"

"Yes. You were lucky. That prof never appears after two o'clock. We do our projects alone. He came by chance just to sit and mark papers." He added, "I, too, am lucky, to find you here. I was 'appy when you escaped."

"I have a child of five who has to be picked up."

"A child?" He said it as though nothing in the world could be as wonderful. I almost fell in love with him at that moment.

"Does he look like you?"

"No, she has blue eye and blond hair, and she's a lot smaller than me."

He smiled. He had slightly curly hair, dark, with some auburn in it, and his top lip, well-shaped, protruded slightly over his lower one. It struck me as a beautiful arrangement.

I asked him if he knew Eugène.

He told me he did and admired him, and thought Sylvie and Patrice amusing. He admitted he was lucky to have many friends at Beaux Arts. Jules was definitely not one of them. "He's a *crétin* and a bore."

I had to leave to pick up Cathy. I rose.

"Wait," he said, and reached in his pocket for a battered notebook with a pencil attached. Half smiling, he asked, "Would you like to meet again sometime?"

Wouldn't I just? I sighed in relief. Thank you, oh thank you, I said silently.

"Yes. I'd like."

"So, if you want, I take you to look at old courtyards in Paris. Some are hidden." He stroked his chin. "Sometimes you may have to run fast, they are actually private, but we go anyway." His eyes twinkled.

"Well, you already know how fast I move."

"I think you possess the prime skills for trespassing," he responded.

After writing down my address, he slipped his notebook into his pocket, flung some coins on the table, and rose, all six feet of him. "Come, Gleene, I'll take you to the bus or the metro or wherever you are going."

Chapter Thirty-six

The day of the trial exams we had the morning free. The night before, however, I sat up for hours cramming, reviewing months of grammar and poetry, and it was while studying the baffling French subjunctive that I fell into a long sleep. I awoke bolt upright, tasting stale coffee and shivering. It was close to three in the morning.

Five hours later, Cathy and I were dipping morsels of baguette into bowls of warm *café au lait*, a treat for her rather than her usual warm milk. I even dipped a sugar lump in my coffee, known as a *"faire un canard,"* and let her carry it from my spoon to her mouth. She sucked it gleefully, noisily *num-yumming*. It amazes me still how this sugar-lump act performed in seconds could provoke such ecstasy.

At school, I watched her push open the front door, then wave to me. After blowing her a kiss, I walked a short way before flopping down on a bench nearby to open my tattered leather volume of poems by Paul Verlaine. Mme Tourdzie idolized this nineteenth-century poet; she could never resist testing us on his asymmetrical verses. I allotted myself an hour for studying, after which I'd take a bus to the Crédit Lyonnais, on the Right Bank, to pick up my monthly check from Joe.

I read the poem again. *"Mon Rêve familier"*—" My Recurring dream." The first lines made me shiver.

Je fais souvent ce rêve étrange et pénétrant
D'une femme inconnue, et que j'aime, et qui m'aime

I often have this strange and penetrating dream
Of an unknown woman, whom I love, and who loves me

When I changed the unknown woman into a man, the immediacy of the poem hit me. It was about Maurice and me. Our time together had been brief, but to me it had been volcanic. When I'd been locked in with those students in that ancient building, I had been comforted by this man's worried expression and assurances that no harm would come to me. Then, after my escape, while we were having coffee together, we seemed to mesh so well. Certainly I was excited by his original mind, his gentle, teasing humor, and his good looks. Then there had been our fifteen-minute walk to the metro, both of us a little drunk with happiness. When we parted, I couldn't stop smiling, knowing I'd be seeing him again soon.

Even before he left me, his blue-green eyes were haunting me.

On the metro I had felt tingling and alive. I listed the reasons why he had stirred me. He'd recently returned from doing volunteer work in South Africa with a team of engineers and biologists. "Our French team there was startled by the new ideas we learned from these so-called primitive villagers," he'd told me. I'd been pleased by his comment.

We had clicked, we had meshed, and he'd sent me a *pneu* asking if I wanted to see him again. I'd sent him one back expressing great interest, but to my surprise he hadn't responded. Had I been too forward? I couldn't understand it. Since we'd met, the sound of his voice filled my ears, and his face would stole across my eyes. In a country famous for love and passion, I pictured how the French would view my impulsive obsession. "Love?" They'd look to the heavens and with their Gallic shrug say, "*C'est simple. Tu l'as dans la peau*"—"It's simple. You've got him under your skin." Did I ever. But why wasn't I under his skin, too?

I caught a bus to the Crédit Lyonnais. Taking a bus in Paris in the fifties was a joy for me. It was considered perfectly fine to goggle at the animated gestures of your fellow passengers and try to decipher snippets of their talk. In a London bus, staring was considered rude. One was rigorously taught never to do it, an admonition at times followed by "Curiosity killed the cat." In Paris, staring seemed quite the thing to do on a bus. Certainly your fellow passengers never hid their curiosity about you.

It was on buses I'd learned, by straining my ears, a few pithy idioms that I could now toss out, as well as a couple of choice insults.

Today, as always, all the marvels of Paris were captured through the dusty bus windows: I looked at the grand buildings and sculptures, the museums and galleries, the glorious bridges spanning the Seine. And for once felt numb to it all. And when the bus turned and I saw a little boy watching a twig flowing in the gutter, it was all I could do not to cry. If only Maurice were beside me.

People everywhere were sitting in outdoor cafes, even now in November. I got off near La Madeleine and entered the bank near the rue Cambon. When I pushed the heavy door on my way out with my stash of francs, I became aware of a handsome man who looked oddly familiar approaching. He was about to pass me. Hurriedly, I held up my hand like a policeman. He stopped.

"*Pardon,*" I said, gaping at him. "*Vous n'êtes pas, par hazard, Jean Gabin?*– "You are not, by any chance, Jean Gabin?"

He bowed and said, "Yes, Mademoiselle, I am the same."

"Goodness! I mean, you do look so much like yourself , as you look in the movies. I've seen all your films—well, most." I tried not to babble, yet my tongue ran on. "They're all superb! The latest, *La Marie du port*—what a gem!" I paused. I realized I sounded gushy, but it was true. "All my friends, we think you're the best actor in France."

He smiled that same smile that had so often melted my heart on the screen, but now was just for me alone. He studied my face for a few moments, then, beaming at me, said, "I would be delighted to make your acquaintance, Mademoiselle. Perhaps you'd like to have a glass of wine with me?"

Oh dear God. Would I ever.

"Golly—" I stopped. Oh darn it, I would love to. "Do you mean right now?"

His blue-gray eyes were irresistible. "There is no time like the present." His voice was gentle and sexy.

"I would dearly love to, but my exam at the Sorbonne, I have to be there in less than a half-hour. If I were absent I'd lose my certification." I was miserable. I tried a more flirtatious tack. "Right now I can't, but . . . "

I was hoping he might to propose a future rendezvous. But I

knew our drink possibility was over by his smile—the irresistible smile from his movies, where he raises one arched eyebrow, ready to back out of a situation.

"*Eh bien*, Mademoiselle, both of us, alas, will regret this lost occasion."

My heart ached as I watched him raise his hat slowly and bow courteously before continuing to walk on in the opposite direction.

Could that be all there was? I turned my head to watch him walk away. Stopping once, he circled about to wave jauntily at me while I was stood glued to the pavement. I hid the disappointment in my face, replacing it with an air of amusement as I waved back at him.

At any rate, the episode made me forget Maurice for the moment. (Of course, the fact that I had this thought showed I hadn't forgotten Maurice at all!) Anyway, it would be fun telling all my friends how Jean Gabin had asked me out. David and Tamara, who never missed one of his films, would be mightily impressed. And I could picture Audrey leaping and screaming. "Glynne! You're mad! I mean, how could you say no?"

Back on the boulevard Saint-Michel, I was heading for the Sorbonne when I heard a deep voice shouting, "Gleene, Gleene!" It was Eugène. He kissed me on each cheek and asked where I'd been hiding. Then he said, "'Remember that guy Maurice, you met at the Beaux Arts? He told me he sent you a *pneu*."

"I answered it with a *pneu* of my own, but he didn't write back."

Eugène raised his palms to the heavens. "Oh Gleene, you cannot send Maurice a *pneu*. They work only within Paris, and he lives in a nearby *départment* called Seine-et-Oise."

A ray of hope started to quiver within me. So this was the explanation for Maurice's not answering my *pneu!*

"Well, now write to him," he said. "But remember, just a regular letter for the postbox, yes?" He was smiling. "And Gleene, would you like to join us, Sylvie, Patrice, and me, next Wednesday at Geneviève for lunch?"

"Dear heavens, yes. Eugène, listen. Actually, I can't talk now, I'm about to take my trials. But thank you. Really, I can never thank you enough for telling me about Maurice not being able to receive *pneus*. It may just solve—oh, everything."

"Excellent. Go now, quick, to your exam," he said.

I kissed his chubby cheeks twice before striding to the long examination room, happier than I'd felt in weeks.

Chapter Thirty-seven

I met Maurice for our first date near the fountain he'd described in his letter, opposite the Comédie-Française. It was dark, and the monument was lit up. I was fascinated by the gorgeous sculpture of a winged nude—a nymph, or an angel perhaps—high up at the pinnacle. Just then, a young man slid down the plane tree behind it. There was Maurice, walking toward me.

We began speaking at the same time and then stopped, both laughing. He covered his mouth with one hand and held out the other to me. It was large and warm.

"I was looking for you from the treetop to find you in case you became lost again." He spoke in French.

"With all your directions, how could I be? Anyway, I actually don't mind getting lost, if it's not for too long a time."

"And, of course, there must be a good ending."

"Above all else." I tried to sound light-hearted yet firm. "Still, I'll never think of my experience at the Beaux Arts as great fun."

"But don't forget, if you had not entered that classroom, we would never have met, so we wouldn't be together tonight."

"True enough."

"Good, that settles it. Tell me, do you mind walking? It will take roughly half an hour to reach the first courtyard."

I never answered his question but found myself walking in step with him, his arm around my shoulders. We took several narrow cobbled streets jammed with other couples and groups of young people, and emerged onto a bright boulevard. After crossing a market square we fell onto a long, quiet street. I was thinking that I could happily travel miles like this when he abruptly stopped before a tall house with a Spanish tiled roof. The house was set behind high wooden siding into which an arched door had been carved. A tiny keyhole was barely visible.

He spoke in English. "It ees here, ze ancient courtyard. With *bonne chance*"— luck—"you will soon see it." He threw me a smile as he took a wafer of flint from his coat pocket, murmuring, "It usually works."

Heavens, I thought, *we'll be trespassing.* Trying not to let him see how scared I felt, I watched him as he eased the flint between his long fingers into the keyhole, then delicately jiggled it. I heard a metallic click, and he quickly pushed open the door with his toe and grabbed my hand to pull me in.

We stepped into the courtyard and were enveloped in a flowery fragrance. Maurice tapped the side of his nose and pointed to the vast clusters of roses hanging all the way up to the top floor. I nodded while taking in the charm and quiet of this hidden kingdom, my earlier fears quite forgotten. In the center of a maze of old brick walkways, jets of water spouted from a few smooth rocks and spilled over into a shallow pool teeming with hundreds of tiny rainbow fish, some of them smaller than bees. To my left stood a life-size stone donkey with soulful eyes. Saddled, it seemed to have been awaiting its rider for years. Here and there over the terracotta tiles were brightly colored flowers in clay pots of every size.

The quiet, heightened by the tinkling water, the perfumed air, and the lonely donkey hinted at another world. But best of all was the sight of Maurice within arm's reach, his face tilted back, staring up. Together we watched a crescent moon sailing in and out of the clouds.

"It's *marrant*, I think, this garden." "Marrant" means appealing and original as well as funny. He faced me, his eyes searching my face. "Do you like ?"

I looked into those amazing eyes of his, eagle-like and blue-green, and all I could come up with was, "It's truly marvelous."

His long fingers pressed mine. "Come on, tell me more," he coaxed. "Why you think it's marvelous?"

My heart was beating fast. I couldn't express anything in a rational way. After the pain of the last weeks, just to be together anywhere with him would have been enough, but to be in this divine courtyard, close enough to breathe in the scent of wool from his jacket, was heaven. I couldn't easily say these words in French or in English. Actually, I hadn't known him long enough for such intimacies.

He was waiting for an answer. God! Why was I so enchanted by the courtyard? And how not to sound trite or gushy? The perfect word leaped into my head, but it was in English, and an odd word, "quiddity"—not in its modern sense of a quibble, but in the sense in which it was used in Medieval scholastic philosophy, of the essential or ultimate form of a thing. I was touched by its being what made it what it was: an old, enchanting courtyard.

Not knowing how to say the word in French, I said, "Well, I love it because each thing, even the fish, tumbling like golden arrows into that big bowl, each thing enhances the whole." How I would have loved to blurt out, "Can't you see, Maurice, I'm in heaven because you're near me?"

He looked keenly at me. "Bravo, Gleene. And how you say it expresses my own feelings, too."

"Thank you," I said. "Maurice, if you promise not to laugh at me, I'm going to make a confession," I said. "For years, I used to try and picture a secret garden where I could curl up undisturbed with a book. The sun would be warm, and nearby on a table would be a bowl of fresh strawberries with sugar and cream. Well, this courtyard could be my imaginary secret garden."

"Yes" he said, "and because it is not your garden nor mine you'll never eat strawberries here—but wherever and whenever you do, eat strawberries, I mean, this place with the donkey may come back to you. It will become your own secret garden, one you can often visit, again and again in your mind."

His eyes were wide and his mouth half-open after he'd stopped speaking and I was trying not to look at the curve on his upper lip, when bingo! Tte spell was broken by an unmistakable American beat. How Parisians loved American jazz! It was Cab Calloway singing the "Chattanooga Choo Choo."

I joined in the chorus. Less than two years ago, I'd danced to this song with Joe's brother Al, the star at every party in Brooklyn.

It was catchy, sensual, and irresistible, so that despite my initial annoyance at the intrusion into our secret garden, my hips were swaying to its rhythms.

Maurice looked as though he wanted to take me in his arms. Pleased, I thought he wanted to dance. He shook his head. "*Non, non, non!* I don't know how to jitterbug. I'll watch you doing it."

I didn't need much urging. My body was jumping inside. I began by tapping my feet in a Lindy step, then I flew around the walkways with funny wiggly steps. Finally I got into the heat of it, dancing fast, sticking out my derriere, turning and twisting. I ended by half-sliding between an invisible Al's legs (who would then have tossed me over his shoulder).

Out of breath I stopped, thankful I hadn't tripped on the moss sprouting up between the old bricks. "Bravo, bravo!" Maurice cried, his eyes wide with admiration. The next thing, I knew I'd landed on his chest. I hid there safely until, cupping my face in his hands, he kissed me. It began as chaste and warm, but I needed more, and soon he was kissing hard, with my mouth responding to his tongue. It was a kiss that went on and on until, in order to breathe, I had to pull away.

I felt faint. We stared at each other for a few seconds, then, very gently, he stroked my cheek with the back of his hand. His eyes seemed inside mine. He spoke slowly, as if dazed. "*Pour moi c'était du tonnere. Et toi?*—"For me that was fantastic. And you?"

I hadn't caught my breath yet, so I just nodded.

He looked at his watch and grimaced. "*Zut*, Gleene! I'm sorry, but we have to go. My last train is at 12:30."

I took a mental picture of the courtyard, blinking two or three times between looks to preserve it, and sniffing the perfumed air. This would be hard to replicate. I said a silent farewell to the swarms of rainbow fish. Maurice patted the donkey's belly, whispering in its ear "*Sois gentil, toi!*"—"Be good!" Then he piloted me back through the small door and pulled it shut behind us.

We were too happy even to talk. My hand wrapped in his felt snug in his jacket pocket, and he was humming an unrecognizable tune. He suddenly pointed to a bus stopped at a light a good distance away. "Gleene, that's ours!" he called out. Holding hands, we ran as fast as we could and reached the bus just as it started picking up speed.

The conductor on the open platform at the back grabbed my hand and pulled me in. Maurice nonchalantly leaped up after me.

"Where did you learn to run like that?" he said, panting . "I could hardly keep up with you."

"On the playing fields in school. Hockey, lacrosse, cricket. Nothing unusual for English girls' public schools."

"In France you never see young women running."

The bus lurched and I was flung against him. I felt the hardness of his thighs, and his arms closed protectively around me. If only the bus would keep lurching!

At that time buses were different, more fun. If you entered in the front, you passed the driver and sat inside. The back was mainly for students, young couples, and teenagers. It was always a thrill for me, riding in the fresh air on a platform that rocked and dipped whenever the bus turned a corner. Maurice stood balanced with his legs apart, not clasping the pole as others were doing, while I held onto his wrist with one hand and the pole with the other. You had to appear unruffled no matter how violently you were hurled about, he explained. If you lost your balance and were about to crash, he thought it permissible to reach up lazily for a pole.

I laughed out loud. "You're joking. You mean there's a sort of bus lore?"

He pursed his curvy lips. "Yes. Not for everybody. Not for the old, children, or women. It's for young men. You'll see lots of them who refuse to walk inside for shelter, even in heavy rain."

"But why?"

"It's from pride. It's acting with a certain panache. So you choose to act in a way you desire rather than give in to the norm."

Mme Tourdzie had said something similar in class as she'd summed up the philosophy of Jean-Paul Sartre, whose works, she said, were now the rage. He espoused existentialism: the bold new belief in man's possibilities, freed from religion, rules, and rituals. I'd read a few of Sartre's works. I said to Maurice, "As Sartre might put it, because we are humans we have in us something different from animals: the freedom to choose."

We had reached our stop. Soon we were devouring almond croissants inside a café with huge glass windows looking onto the street. We had only a few minutes to talk. Maurice tried to clarify his predicament about dancing. I knew it would take him three times longer to say in English than in French, but there was no tactful way of interrupting him. Finally I caught his wrist and tapped his watch. He looked down and shook his head. "*Oh là-là! On dirait que je ne suis pas très pratique.*"—"I'm not very practical." He flung some coins on the table and stood up.

He reclaimed our hand arrangement, his over mine, for our final trot. We clattered down the stone steps to the metro and saw his train waiting, its double doors still open. He planted a fast kiss on my lips and jumped in. His hair was tousled from running. How young he looked! Then I felt a sinking in my stomach: he had not invited me for another rendezvous.

He stood facing me in the door. "Answer me before I disappear," he said. Relief washed over me, but too soon. "Have you ever heard of *Le Petit Prince?*"

"No. Is it a film?" I asked, my happiness gone.

"Not yet! I'm sure it will be."

"Keep clear of the doors," the stationmaster announced.

I stared at him helplessly through the glass doors. He seemed to be pulling strange faces. I moved closer until my nose was nearly touching the glass. He was mouthing exaggeratedly. Reading his lips, the message was, "Same place, same time, next week. Understand?"

My head bounced, nodding with relief.

I shouted back to him as the train started moving, "Yes! I'll be there."

Chapter Thirty-eight

After a week of changing my mind about what to wear for my second date with Maurice, I decided not to wear the red blouse topped with the white shawl, the one Tamara had crocheted for me during her pregnancy. Although Cathy, pushing her fingers through its loopy holes and waggling them, insisted it looked lovely on me, I knew better.

No matter which way it was arranged, it ruled out any possibility of "femme fatale."

The white shawl had given Cathy a hunched allure when she'd played Grandma in Little Red Riding Hood. This was a great secret she'd kept for days, a surprise for me when I saw the performance. She was no longer just a tree: she had a speaking role as Grandma!

Now I lay the shawl down and grabbed my purple sweater to replace the red one I'd worn last time and the same gray skirt.. The salesgirl had pronounced it *ravissante* on me. That had done the trick. In the small shop I'd examined myself frontways and then strained my neck trying to glimpse something of my posterior. The salesgirl had smiled, pointing to my hips, and said, *"Ah! Superbe!"* Her French pronunciation of "superb" was deliciously elongated. After an admiring pause, she'd added, "I tell you why. For the hips, it is cut on the bias, to enhance them while giving flowing to your walk."

She'd twirled her fingers on high to draw the outline of a pear. Heavens, I'd thought, so young yet so knowledgeable. Although not yet twenty, this French girl knew all about seduction in the cut. But then she was a Parisian—a young *demoiselle* living in the fashion capital of the world. If she didn't know about couture then who did? Holding my package, I'd walked into the street, reliving the word she had pronounced: *ravissante.*

But this wasn't the moment for day-dreaming. I'd have to make tracks to get to Maurice on time. I decided on my spring coat even though it was wintry outside because it was more sophisticated than my bulky winter jacket, which Maurice had already seen.

Cathy sat cross-legged in the living room in her pajamas. She was arranging her favorite nursery rhyme records one on top of the other on her small Victrola, to which she would sing in her piping voice alongside Mme Doucet's baritone after I'd left the house. "I'm not putting on 'Frère Jacques,'" she announced firmly. "How I used to love that song when I was little!" She shrugged, the French way, her palms facing up, pouting. *"Eh bah, tout change!"*—"Oh well, everything changes!" She looked up at me. "Where are you going tonight?"

"I don't know, sweetheart. The cinema, or perhaps the theatre. I'm meeting a friend of the friends I eat lunch with at Geneviève. A man called Maurice."

"Do you think Maurice likes children?" she asked.

"He won't be coming back here," I said, hastily. "But, yes, I think so."

"Does he like to play games with them, like Ned?"

"Stop, darling, I'm late, and I'm not ready."

"But does he?"

I thought of Maurice's playfulness with me. "Well, more than likely." I knew she was thinking up more questions, so I added quickly, "I'll tell you more tomorrow."

When I came back into the living room, Mme Doucet stopped to look me up and down.

"Is that how you're going to your rendezvous? No earrings? No necklace?" There was a pause, then she added, "Not that you look too bad."

I thanked her for the dubious compliment. Madame, who always dressed in regalia— brooches, earrings, and satin scarves— simply to cross the street to the bakery, seemed genuinely perplexed by my lack of ornamentation.

At any rate, it didn't bother me. I was full of nervous excite-

ment. The thought that I'd soon be seeing Maurice made my insides thud. I took a few gulps of air to steady myself before turning
to Cathy, who'd asked patiently, "*Maman*, can't you hear me? I
said, 'is it all right if we sing five songs, Madame and me, before
I sleep?'"

"Well, no more than five," I said firmly, which triggered her to
shout, "Ten! Ten songs, *Maman*!" She held her arms around me,
gently tickling my neck before I left.

The first sight of Maurice outside the Comédie-Française made
me nearly faint. I sensed that he was excited, too.

"Aah! Gleene, I have a surprise for you." After a short kiss,
he searched my face, his eyes wide as a cat's. He had one hand
around my waist; the other held a small package wrapped in blue
paper. Releasing me, he stepped back, holding out the package,
half smiling. "You will like him, I think. *Non, non,* I mean like it, I
think." He gave a comical pout at his error.

I opened the paper carefully and saw it was a book, *Le Petit
Prince.*

"Oh, Maurice! I swallowed. "What a wonderful surprise."

I shook my head, knowing what hardcover books like this cost.
And for Maurice, who worked nights after school, this had to have
been a splurge. "Really, you shouldn't have," I said, adding, "but
I'm absolutely delighted."

He looked pleased. "I was searching for something authentical-
ly French for you. Many people think this book is just for children,
but it isn't. It's for all ages. In some ways 'Le Petit Prince' is like
Alice in Wonderland,'" he said. "To me it will always be funny and
marvelous, even when I'm ninety."

I tried not to smile., "Perhaps it will be even better in one's dot-
age," I said, stealing a glance at him. I held up the book, taking in
the drawing of the yellow-haired prince's quixotic expression. His
royal mantle seemed too big for him.

"This picture of him on the cover is charming. Is the Prince the
son of the king of a country?" I asked.

"In a way, he himself is the sovereign of his own planet. But it
is a planet without any citizens, since he's the only person living
on it."

"Oh." I tried to digest this.

He dropped my hand and jumped ahead to face me. "Gleene, listen, it's important for you to know that the author was actually in real life a pilot. In France today he's a kind of hero. His name is Antoine de Saint-Exupéry."

We resumed walking, my hand in his again.

Maurice continued, "His life and his death are clouded in mystery. One day in 1944, on a routine mission, he just disappeared. His plane, too, was never seen again. Some think he is still somewhere in the clouds. Others are convinced he has landed on another planet." Maurice raised his brows, half shrugging. "I think one day we will discover what happened. Perhaps not in our lifetime."

"Well, I can't wait to read it."

"You 'ave not to wait," Maurice said, pulling me down onto a bench under a lamppost.

We sat close, his hip touching mine. I thought he was about to kiss me. Instead, he opened the book with reverence. Then, taking one of my hands in his, he began reading. His Parisian French rose and fell seductively, making it hard for me not to fling my arms around his neck.

He paused for a minute and said in English, "I read much of this part to explain you 'ow it 'appened." His eyes were piercing mine. "Don't be impatient, Gleene. You'll find out everything in the end." Was he thinking of reading me the entire book? My heart sank. He flipped through a some pages and read aloud slowly, pausing for a private chuckle. He stopped abruptly, patting my shoulder to ask, "Gleene—do you understand me when I read?"

His voice thrilled me, and I understood most of the words as he uttered them. But did I understand the sense? Not really. In fact, listening to his voice spiraling up into the night air had become quite sleep-provoking. I was worried I might nod off. And then— while parts of the book seemed quaint, humorous even, the story seemed a patchwork of sorts.

"Well, umm, mostly," I said, although in truth it had become less comprehensible.

Dessine moi un mouton" or "Draw me a sheep" the little prince asks the pilot. I didn't want to ask why the little prince would ask the pilot to draw him a sheep just when the pilot has crashed onto the prince's planet and our poor pilot has not eaten for days. Why didn't the golden-haired prince offer him something to eat instead? My stomach began to lurch. I foresaw the whimsy might entirely elude me. One thing that seemed wearisome—though I guessed Maurice and I might disagree on the matter—was the pilot's oft-repeated "wisdom" that grown-ups don't understand certain things.

Perhaps being chilly had prejudiced me, too. I was numb with cold. Wistful thoughts of the bulky jacket I'd left home interfered with my concentration.

Maurice, totally fascinated, went on reading, pausing only to ask if I knew what "*apprivoiser*" meant. When I shook my head, he began to explain in his limited English. "Think of a lion, um, attender. 'E has to take care of him because it belongs to 'im. You see?"

I was lost, irrevocably. I managed a polite "Oh!"

He returned to his reading, a smile hovering on his lips. Finally, my teeth began to chatter.

Maurice looked up suddenly to explain, "You see, it was 'is rose so 'e 'ad to care for what 'appened to it."

"Oh, really," was all I could say.

Maurice leaped up. "*Zut!* Gleene. But you are frozen." Enfolding me in his arms and pressing me to his chest he said, "But why didn't you say something? He opened his jacket, folding it around me. "*Viens, petite fille,*" he said. "We're going to a restaurant nearby. You're freezed because you're hungry."

We crossed to a restaurant called Le Cochon Engraissé—The Fatted Hog. Inside it was dense with blue smoke, noisy but wonderfully warm. The place was packed.

A robust gray-haired man approached. Maurice greeted him affably. "*Bonsoir*, Raoul."

"Don't worry, Monsieur Maurice, we'll fit you in." He motioned to two workers at the bar who soon arrived with a table, which they set down in front. A white-aproned waiter deftly flung a checkered tablecloth across it.

So side by side, the two of us faced the wide glass front, through which some of the lit-up street was visible. We'd walked a distance to get here, and now both of us relaxed, We concentrated on the handwritten menu. They were hand written and included a smudge or two.

When I looked up, Maurice's eyes were laughing. "Poor freezed little girl!" He took one of my hands. "There you were an icicle on the bench, not once complaining." He scrutinized my face. "But why, why for the love of god, didn't you tell me 'I am freezed'?" He shook his head and squeezed my hand as we took up our menus again. "This place is not renowned for *le chic*," Maurice said, but it is known for *la briffe*."

I wondered what part of the pig *la briffe* was.

Maurice poured wine from a large carafe. "Gleene," he ordered, "make a toast."

I wanted to drink to love, but I thought he might feel I was rushing things. Yet for the first time in my life, I felt I really was in love. I raised my glass. "To Paris," I said.

I went back to studying my menu. "Maurice, I can't find *la briffe* on the menu."

Maurice's mouth twitched. "*La briffe* is not the name of a dish. It's something like *la bouffe*, a slang term for "food." "Briffe" is high slang—Parisian."

The young waiter, nearby with his pad, laughed before mumbling an apology.

Without a glance at the menu, Maurice ordered. "For both of us, the loin of pork stuffed with prunes and apricots." He added, "With the hope that the chef hasn't tried to improve his sauce."

"Monsieur, rest assured it is as always." He touched his lips then tossed his fingers up: "Perfection."

He returned with two steaming plates, cautioning, "*Touchez pas. C'est chaud!*"—"Don't touch. It's hot!"

Oh glory! That first mouthful! The meat, impregnated with the fantastic sauce, was pure joy. There seemed to be so many different flavors on my palate. Exchanging greedy looks of delight, we dug in. When the last morsel had disappeared from Maurice's plate, I watched how he broke off bits of baguette and tossed them onto his plate, then mopped up the gravy. Throwing my English etiquette to the winds, I did likewise.

Suddenly a radiant young woman stopped in front of our table, flung her arms around Maurice's shoulders, and planted a long kiss on his mouth.

A worm crawled through my stomach.

Maurice had swiftly removed the arms of this goddess, but she was undeterred. Her eyes sparkled as she said, "I saw you through the window. Why haven't you come to my studio? It's been months!"

Not answering, Maurice made introductions. "Gleene, meet Bunny. She's a talented designer of carpets. And Gleene is an English student at the Sorbonne getting her certificate."

Bunny barely glanced at me. "Aren't you coming to see my latest works? They are, if I do say so myself, really bold."

Bold and bratty, like you, I thought.

"Remember the advice you gave me last time?" she continued. "It was because of you, Maurice, that I won two prizes. I would never have chosen the ones you selected. I need you to advise me again." Her eyes were beckoning, flirtatious. "Don't let me down. I expect to see you, very soon, *mon chéri*. Excuse me for now; I really must go. As usual, I'm terribly late for a rendezvous."

As she turned to leave, it seemed that everyone in the place was watching our scene with interest, especially when Bunny bent forward to whisper something in Maurice's ear while stroking his cheek. Finally she left.

Maurice was pale. "Look," he said, "it is no need to explain you this... but it is your right to know." Wanting me to understand, he spoke a mixture of English and French. "Obviously Bunny is beautiful, but I don't have the least desire for her. There's nothing between us except her carpet designs."

My throat was parched. I sipped some wine.

"More than a year ago we had a very brief affair. Two nights. She has a lot of sex appeal, but she's *casse-pieds*"—a pain in the neck."

Could I believe him? How could any fellow not be attracted to that stunning face, that sexy body, the energy that Bunny radiated?

"Although I think she still wants me, I don't want her. Gleene, please believe me."

I felt a trickle of something like relief warming my body.

"I've tried to discourage her," he said. "For me, there is no possibility of a relationship with her." His hand was resting lightly on my shoulder, his eyes serious.

The restaurant was emptying out. I was desperately relieved by his rejection of Bunny. It seemed a miracle, yet I sensed he was telling the truth. I reached over and laid my hand on top of his; he cupped his other hand over mine. We stayed like that until the waiter arrived with the bill.

Near his train station, Maurice told me that a friend of his, Arianne, a psychoanalyst, was giving a soirée on Thursday evening and that he'd pick me up at seven at my place, since the party was near me.

"*Au revoir* until Thursday, Gleene, my lovely one."

In five days I'd be seeing him again. My body began singing. His mouth pressed hard on mine, our tongues touching for a few perfect seconds. I tasted again the sauce on his lips before he sped away.

Chapter Thirty-nine

As we climbed the four flights to my apartment after the party, I caught a whiff of Maurice's tweed jacket, damp and masculine. The staircase was narrow, and Maurice led the way, holding my hand. He'd turn to ask a question or to grin, and I was conscious of the sexual charge between us. He gave me a kiss, which caught me off balance, and I nearly tripped, but in seconds he caught my shoulder. Hanging onto him as well as the banister, I heard him shout, " Gleene, *bon dieu*, are you okay?" My heart was beating fast in my ears. It had been a close shave— I'd have fallen down a half flight of stairs.

With both feet at last on the same step, I shook each leg before answering. "Fine, I'm fine. Yes, really."

He shook a cautionary finger at me. *"Gleene, c'est finis. Plus s'embrasser sur l'escalier!"* From now on, no more kissing on the stairs! Our laughter echoed noisily up and down the stone steps.

Abruptly, a door opened below us, and a woman in a bathrobe peered up. "Do you have any idea what time it is?" Her voice was filled with repressed anger. "You're not only waking my kids, but the entire house. How dare you be so thoughtless?" She was trying to control her fury. "A little consideration, surely!"

Maurice's laughter froze. He made the Gallic gesture of half-biting his forefinger to admit his mistake, and when he answered her, his voice was subdued. "Please accept our sincere apologies, Madame. We just lost track of things." She sniffed and closed the door.

His finger near his mouth, Maurice whispered, "We'd better ooosht. Quiet. Everything sounds louder at night. We may have awoken up the whole house. Possibly even your landlady!"

My smile evaporated. God! Just suppose she 'd be there to meet us upstairs. I had a vision of her with her sly, know-it-all expression, addressing questions to Maurice, her voice unctuous, demanding. "What year, Monsieur, did you say, are you in with your studies at the École des Beaux Arts?"

When we reached our landing, I turned the heavy key in the lock. I exhaled and danced a mental jig. "Come in. The coast's clear," I whispered to him.

"Aah. Madame sleeps?"

"Let's hope."

"And Cathy?"

"With my friends Tamara and David.

Conspirators, we tiptoed into my bedroom and closed the door quietly. We stood near the bed kissing for a long time, until he said, "You must be frozen! Let's get undressed. We'll warm up under the covers."

All along, I'd been nerve-wracked about Maurice seeing my breasts. Would he be put off? They were at least twice the size of the average French girl's, and they seemed at their biggest when first released from their moorings, tumbling out in all their fullness. To avoid shocking him, I'd planned to nip into the bathroom with my nightdress in hand. There I'd undo my bra and slip on the nightie before returning.

But it was too late now. He was pulling off his clothes fast. As I started to unzip my skirt, Maurice came behind me and tugged off my sweater, and the next thing I knew, he was unfastening my bra.

He spun me around to face him, his eyes moving over my body. There was a small silence. Heavens! Was he shocked? Then he said, "Gleene, *que tu es belle. Si belle. Tu es ravissante.*"—"Glynne, how beautiful you are. So beautiful. You are ravishing."

He pushed me gently toward the bed and I watched him, naked, as he grabbed the heavy draperies and dragged them across the windows. His physique surprised me. He always wore roomy shirts or loose sweaters, mostly covered by an unbuttoned jacket. I'd noted his strong forearms when he'd rolled up his sleeves, and from the start I'd enjoyed the nonchalant spring of his walk. But now, his smooth-muscled arms and legs, not to mention the firm, rounded buttocks, started a pounding in my head.

He turned and came toward me, his penis full and high. In seconds I was lying under him, his blue-green eyes searching mine. Neither of us spoke. His arm reached out to turn off the small bed lamp, then he changed his mind. "We need to see each other, yes?"

Did we? I wasn't sure.

Then time was replaced by another dimension, until I was abruptly awakened by piercing cries, like seagulls shrieking. I felt fingers cover my dry mouth, "Oooosht! Oooosh! *Ma chérie!* You'll awaken Madame." His eyes smiled into mine and then he moved onto his side, closing himself comfortably around my body. "Sleep," he ordered. I leaned into his body, listening to his breath against my ear. Then I lost consciousness.

When I awoke at dawn, he was standing at the window watching the sun rise, pearly pink and mauve.

"*Bonjour,*" I said.

He came back to bed, then asked, "Would you like to hear a French song? Remember, I never sing in key."

I nodded and he sang something sad about a prisoner in a tower.It had nothing to do with me or him, but it made me want to cry, without understanding why. The tune was haunting, and I'd never forget it.

Then it was my turn. "I'll recite two lines from a poem by William Wordsworth. It's about the French Revolution, but it expresses what I feel at this exact moment."

Bliss it was in that dawn to be alive
But to be young was very heaven.

"*Quest-ce que c'est* 'blees'?" he asked

"Watch," I said. I closed my eyes, threw back my head, and ecstatically took in deep breaths.

"*Ah! Je comprend. Le ravissement, ou bien l'extase.*"—I understand. Rapture, or ecstasy.

His lips, taut yet velvety, met mine. Then his whole tongue entered my mouth for a few seconds.

"That's how I feel, too," he said. We smiled at each another. "Now tell me," he said, teasing, "tell me how you feel this minute."

I smiled lazily.

He pushed me down.

Afterward, he asked, seriously, "Gleene, you thought perhaps all these weeks, maybe I wasn't, umm, capable, that I couldn't perform? Is that true?"

"Not exactly," I said. "But it was strange. You seemed attracted to me but we were never alone indoors."

He gave a small bark of amusement. "But you know I live with my mother."

"Why did you never ask to come upstairs with me?"

"I couldn't make love with you because Cathy might hear us."

"But late at night she's asleep."

"Perhaps." He threw me a sly look. "But, you especially know"— his eyes were laughing—"there are often noises and cries. She could awaken terrified. I wouldn't feel at ease."

He's more decent than I am, I thought.

"And what do you think your Cathy is doing right now? At your friends' house?"

"Well, she could be braiding the wispy hairs on their new baby's head, tying them with colored ribbons. Or she could be crooning nursery rhymes to the baby. Cathy's never bored."

"And you?

"Too busy with classes, with Cathy, and so many things to do in Paris, and often in such good company." I looked at him.

"Now, Gleene, I will take you for a marvelous breakfast. Not just croissants and coffee, but an American breakfast of omelets, ham, strawberries and *frites*. But you get this breakfast on one condition." His piercing gaze swept over my body, then slowly came back to my face. "You must answer truthfully. At this minute, is there anything you would prefer to a perfectly cooked breakfast?"

Stroking his cheek, I pretended to consider. "And you?"

"Yes," he said. "I'd much prefer to do something else."

Our clothes lay in a heap on the carpet. Our bed was still warm. His face was touching mine, his voice low. "I can't let you go," he said.

Abruptly, I thought of Michelangelo's statue of David, hero of the David and Goliath bible story. Somehow the artist had caught the vulnerable nudity of the young man as he was about to fight the armored giant Goliath. In his bent arm he holds a small sling of pebbles.

"What are you thinking, Gleene?" Maurice asked. "Answer."

I felt his warm hands moving down my limbs and totally forgot the David statue.It was lunchtime before we embarked on our huge American breakfast, gobbling it down with bowls of *café au lait,* happy in our new intimacy. We talked about how the Greeks in the Golden Age admired intelligence more than brute strength, which was why they made a hero out of David, a lad of eighteen who took careful aim at the one bare spot in Goliath's armor, his forehead, before slinging the pebble that killed his enemy.

"I know only a few Bible stories," Maurice said, "but as a child, this one always made me happy. There was a picture in my book of their armies jeering at the sight of a naked boy against the six-foot-tall Goliath—until *bong!* The giant falls dead. There's a picture of David, after having wrapped up his pebbles, quietly walking away to become King of Israel."

If only, I thought, we could go on like this. Or, at the very least, I could spend one more year in Paris. But there was no way. Joe had recently written that he wanted to see Cathy, and if I didn't return to the U.S. he had the legal right to take her from me.

Now that I'd found love at last it came with a deadline. In three months I would have to return to the States.

Chapter Forty

Over the following weeks I met Maurice's friends—architects, students, and painters—and became close to two pals of his, Arianne and Claude. Over time, they became my dearest companions. How lucky I was to be accepted by these accomplished young women! Although I was slightly in awe of their sophistication and encyclopedic knowledge, we came together through storytelling and laughter. Even their gossip seemed richer than the usual stuff. I tried to imitate their way of interpreting stories as they talked, gesturing with their hands. Through them I learned of holidays I'd not been aware of, such as the first of May, when a young man gives a bunch of lily of the valley to his sweetheart. Or the Bal de la Ste-Catherine, on November 25, when young single women wear gorgeous flowered hats they've made to show that they're looking for a husband.

They also filled me in on what's done or not done in Paris—*ce qu'il faut et ce qu'il ne faut pas faire.*

Arianne, the psychoanalyst, had fascinated me from the start, when she'd opened the door to Maurice and me and pulled us into her noisy flat, her party in full swing. She was blond and petite, and her frankness disarmed me. After pecking Maurice's cheeks several times, she beamed at me, saying in passable English, "Gleene, I want to meet you before, but Maurice want you all to himself!"

Claude, immaculately coiffed in a sleek short cut, seemed somewhat formidable at first. She presided over a top agency for engineers, sometimes dating those she fancied. All this, and only a couple of years older than I was! Her sophistication and clever retorts were balanced by honesty and warmth.

When Arianne said goodbye, she unexpectedly held me at arm's length and asked me if I wanted to have tea with her and Claude the following week.

I nodded vigorously.

"Five o'clock Thursday at Le Salon de Marie, okay?"

"I look forward to it."

Maurice said, "Am I excluded?"

Arianne gave him a look. "Of course! How can we talk about you if you're with us?"

At the Salon, we talked with an airy sort of candor as we munched heavenly chestnut cakes and drank tea. Arianne asked us which attribute in a man would suffice to sweep us off our feet.

She started things rolling by saying, "Despite my air of self-sufficiency, what I crave is a mercilessly masculine type. Someone to call all the shots. No beating, mind you—or, if so, only gently."

Claude wanted a man a year or two older, one who was even more intelligent than she was. Above all, he had to be sure of himself in bed—a man who'd know without being told just how to please her.

It was my turn. I was hesitant. "I'm not sure exactly what sweeps me off my feet—"

Arianne interrupted. "That's okay, we know. It's a guy called Maurice!"

"And it's understandable," said Claude. "He's marvelous. He's a romantic. I suspect you are, too." She smiled sympathetically.

"Gleene," Arianne went on, "don't laugh! Pay attention. Romantics continue their whole life searching for the unattainable. They're like Peter Pan. They don't want to grow up."

"Oh, be reasonable, Arianne," Claude broke in. "Maurice is much more than a simple romantic. Didn't I almost fall in love with him, before Edmondo? Maurice is the kind of a dreamer who pulls you into his orbit. But he's also a hard worker. And remember, he's been a loyal friend to me and to you."

"Maurice should really be a poet," said Arianne.

"But he is, " I insisted.

The chimes of a distant clock stopped me. Time to fetch Cathy. Where had the time gone? I told them I had to dash.

"How about Thursday next week?" Arianne asked. "Same time, same place."

We all agreed.

It was the French who came up with the expression *idée fixe*, and it seemed made for Maurice. He had the fixed idea that all young men and women were attracted to one another. "*C'est normale*," he said—"It's only natural."

"But, Maurice, there's more to it," I responded. "Those mild flirtations, say, a stranger looking into your eyes, or semi-seductive conversations with classmates, are fine. They make one feel good, and they're harmless since they're transient, so quickly forgotten."

"Yes, but why should we forget them? We can so easily prevent having babies nowadays." He said it teasingly.

"You know what I think?" I replied. "You like to do what in English we call playing devil's advocate, taking a position for its own sake, rather than questioning its validity."

"Ah yes," he said. "We have that in French as well— *se faire l'avocat du diable.*"

"And, in your case," I continued, "you forget that at heart you're a total romantic."

He raised his eyebrows.

"Just think of your favorite books," I insisted, "like *Le Grand Meaulnes*. Can anything be more romantic than a seventeen-year-old boy's obsession for the girl of his dreams? Or *Le Petit Prince*. What touched you most was how the Prince took care of his rose despite the thorns that tore his fingers. He loved it because it was the one living thing on his planet besides himself."

Our conversations rarely reached conclusions. They usually ended with one of Maurice's elliptical remarks, said with a smile.

"Perhaps it's not a matter of right or wrong. It's normal to feel love for one person even while appreciating the charms of another? Don't you agree?"

I nodded. Was it because he was handsome, or was it his old-fashioned courtesy that made Maurice so appreciated by women? I, too, had been similarly bowled over by him that very first time he had found me in the café. After we parted, my body had shivered with excitement all the way home, knowing I'd be seeing him again.

And here we were facing each other, a couple of months later, sitting on the damp grass on the Île Saint-Louis on a warm spring afternoon. Maurice had agreed to give his opinion of my recitation of the poem I'd chosen for my oral finals in literature. He'd promised to have a heart of stone and pounce on even the most trivial mispronunciation.

When he learned that I'd chosen "Barbara" by Jacques Prévert, he'd raised his brows in disbelief. He was amazed that the judges, "*les grise-barbes*," students called them—graybeards— would think of accepting a poem by a contemporary poet, especially one who was the rage of Paris.

I explained that "Le Maître," the head of the poetry department, had suggested that I recite something more traditional. I told him that what I really loved about "Barbara" was that it made me think as well as cry.

To my surprise, he responded, "You are not wrong, Mademoiselle. For a poem to succeed, it needs its readers to respond to it emotionally as well as intellectually." He threw me a searching look. "But a more important question: Why this particular poem?"

"It's about our world. A once-beautiful town, Brest, is reduced to muck and rubble by the War. The senselessness and stupidity of war overwhelmed me," I ended, choked up.

Le Maître wrote something on his pad, saying he was giving his permission to allow me to recite "Barbara." He tore off the sheet of paper and handed it to me. "Better hold onto this when you go in for your orals," he said, smiling. Then he shook my hand. "I wish you the best of luck, Mademoiselle."

"Lucky for you Le Maître happened to be *un type chic*," Maurice said. "I doubt the rest of the committee will applaud your choice of poem." He shook his head. "I think what really happened is you captivated Le Maître as you do so many others. He couldn't refuse you! So are you ready to recite?"

"I'm ready. Every night before falling asleep these past weeks I've recited this poem. It will be in my head forever."

I stood up. Keeping my back straight, I announced, "'*Bar-ba-ra*,' *par Jacques Prévert*." Then, pushing my lips into a slight

French pout, I began speaking loudly and clearly.

I stopped only once, after the line "*Quelle connerie la guerre*"—"what idiocy war is." I knew I'd sounded too emotional.

I felt nervous. I looked at Maurice questioningly. His mouth was slightly open and he was staring at me, half-smiling.

"Well? Say something, Maurice!"

"*Oh là-là! Bravo!* You didn't stumble or forget one word. And it's a long poem."

"Heavens! Really?"

"Just one small thing, *chérie*. "*Connerie*" is a vulgar word, so it needs a harsher sound than the way you said it. Remember, Prévert is very angry."

I tried it several times until he shouted "*Ça y est!*"—"That's it!" After which there was a silence, and he said, "And you know . . . "

I waited. "What? What else needed fixing?"

"Nothing, Gleene. You're perfect. And . . . " He was struggling to speak.

"Lord, what on earth is it?"

"*Je t'aime Gleen*"—"I love you."

Paralyzed with joy, I was unable to smile. I wanted to run in circles, to laugh and cry. Instead, banalities flew out of my mouth. "Oh God, Maurice, I can't believe it. Do you have any idea how much I love you—have loved you—but was unable able to tell you? Did you never guess?"

"Of course I knew," he said. He pulled me down on the grass next to him, his eyes searching mine.

"I have one year more at the Beaux Arts, and, alas, little money. I can't offer you very much. When you return to the United States, I'll miss you. We have only a few weeks left in Paris to be together."

I knew it was out of the question for him to follow me to New York. He'd be a fish out of water in the U.S. And as deeply as I loved him and Paris, I also longed to hear English spoken all around me again, even if the accent was American.

"I'll come back to Paris and visit you," I said in a small voice.

"You must to do that often. And I'll always be here for you. Nothing will change." He looked as solemn as I felt.

I nodded, tears in my eyes.

We resolved then and there to spend every spare minute together until it was time for me to leave. Since Cathy was spending the month with her ten-year-old cousin in the mountains, Maurice I and would have a lot of time to be alone together.

We made good use of the time. Maurice visited me early every evening and slept over. After he'd had a snack, we'd make love. Sometimes he'd begin by snuffling like a dog, his mouth in my neck. I wasn't sure if I liked this, but I didn't want to spoil his pleasure. And once he stopped snuffling, our love-making was as wonderful as ever. Before I'd reach climax, he'd often pull out his penis, waiting for me to cry, "Put it back, quick!" which is what he did, and we would both climax profoundly, together, moaning. Afterwards we'd fall asleep, with him curled around me.

I was amazed at how often, totally exhausted, we would begin all over again in a couple of hours.

Chapter Forty-one

I did return often to Paris, and it was always beautiful. But it was never quite like my Paris of the fifties. In the two years I'd spent there, I'd made hard decisions, mastered a new language, made several lifelong friends, and even acquired a new passport photo! And I'd brought up a happy little girl. She remains my dearest companion.

As for love, I had been smitten by dear, laconic Ned. His wonderful laugh cannot be erased. But it was Maurice, the sensitive, poetic lover—at some times tempestuous, at others slightly mocking, and everlastingly curious—who showed me how to love one man forever.

I said good-bye to my friends. Arianne slipped a necklace of pale azure stones around my neck, and Claude gave me golden earrings. Tamara and David took me and Maurice to a superb dinner at a posh restaurant.

"Yes, you'll go back to America," Maurice said. "And I'll be in Paris. But I will be here for you always whenever you return. And Gleene, because we love each other, you'll come back often."

I did, of course. And it was always magical with him.

Chapter Forty-two

Thirty-five years later, Cathy and I were looking at old photographs in my house in Larchmont, New York. Cathy was now married, with three children of her own, and I was married to my third husband, Brian. Maurice had died of a heart attack seven years earlier, at the appallingly young age of fifty-six. I've never gotten over his death.

Cathy scrutinized a black-and-white photo with old-fashioned, scalloped edges taken of me and her and Joe sitting at an outdoor table shortly after we'd landed in Cannes. She said, "I can't believe I was so blonde!"

"You looked like a little angel," I told her. Now her hair was brown and wavy.

She pulled out another photograph, a headshot of Maurice, with his sensitive eyes, elegant bone structure, and sculptured mouth. Cathy said, "He really was a beautiful man."

"So much more than that!" I told her. "He was charming and whimsical and able to love like no other."

We were silent for a while. Then I said, "You know, I've had a life filled with love and romance. And I've had great times with many men. But there's one thing I'm absolutely sure of. From the bottom of my heart, I think I loved Maurice."

Cathy burst out laughing.

"What? What's so funny?"

"Oh, Mom. From the bottom of your heart, you *think* you loved Maurice?"

Fin

About the Author

Glynne Hiller, now 94, received her B.A. and her M.A. from Manhattanville College. The author of two books on teenage health and beauty, Glynne is an authority on the French writer, Colette. Glynne has published pieces about Colette in the *New York Times Magazine* and *The Nation*, and she named her younger daughter "Colette." For many years, Glynne taught courses on Colette, Proust, and Virginia Woolf at Manhattanville College and the New School in New York City.

Married three times, Glynne has lived in Manchester, England; Paris; Greenwich Village; Park Slope, Brooklyn; and Larchmont, New York. She currently resides in Sag Harbor, New York, where she enjoys long walks on the beach and cups of tea with friends.

CPSIA information can be obtained
at www.ICGtesting.com
Printed in the USA
FFOW03n1156290418
46403542-48182FF